THE BEST CANADIAN POETRY IN ENGLISH 2009

The Best
Canadian Poetry
in English

2009

Edited by

A.F. Moritz

Series Editor

Molly Peacock

Tightrope Books

Tightrope Books
602 Markham Street
Toronto, Ontario
Canada M6G 2L8
www.tightropebooks.com

EDITOR: A.F. Moritz
SERIES EDITOR: Molly Peacock
MANAGING EDITOR: Heather Wood
COPY EDITOR: Shirarose Wilensky
COVER ART: Shelley Adler
COVER DESIGN: Karen Correia Da Silva
BOOK DESIGN: Carlton Wilson
TYPESETTING: Shirarose Wilensky

Produced with the support of the Canada Council for the Arts and the Ontario Arts Council.

Printed in Canada.

LIBRARY AND ARCHIVES CANADA CATALOGUING IN PUBLICATION

The best Canadian poetry in English, 2009 / editor: A.F. Moritz.

ISBN 978-1-926639-03-1

1. Canadian poetry (English)–21st century. I. Moritz, A.F.

PS8293.1.B48 2009   C811'.608   C2009-903917-6

CONTENTS

Contents

Welcome to our second volume in the ongoing *The Best Canadian Poetry in English* series. These fifty zesty, meditative, funny, philosophical, personal, familiarly strange and strangely familiar poems offer more proof that outstanding poetry of huge variety thrives in Canada. Last year, our inaugural effort, edited by the perspicacious Stephanie Bolster, was a success beyond our wildest dreams—both in sales and in cultural impact. Bolster's intelligent choices and steady hand inaugurated a series that has not only been well received by the poetry world, but, most importantly, by the general public. *The Best Canadian Poetry in English 2008* was launched in Vancouver, Toronto, New Brunswick, and Montreal and was subsequently an Indigo pick for Poetry Month, distributed across the country, received into the hands of readers greedy for experiences that are brief, intense, explosive, and lyrical—often in the same package.

A.F. Moritz, Griffin Prize-winning, internationally regarded poet, is our 2009 guest editor. Moritz read fifty-four literary magazines over the year and agonized over the possible choices. From these he selected the longlist of 100 poems. Moritz is convinced that the poetry published in Canadian literary journals this year is stellar; as a result he found his decisions heart-wrenching to make. The 100 poems that comprise the shortlist and the longlist could almost have been divided into two stunning anthologies. That's the reason, as series editor, I'm committed to including in this anthology the titles of poems and the poets on *The Best Canadian Poetry in English* longlist. The additional fifty poems show poetry's vital reach across the country, demonstrating the depth and range of aesthetic approaches among poets and literary journals in Canada today. To be chosen in the top 100 from among thousands of possible candidates is significant, especially to emerging poets, and gratifying to those literary magazine editors who constantly look for talent. One of our most revered poets, P.K. Page, thanked us for her place on last year's longlist. Perhaps the experience of her years has shown her the exigencies of excellence—or the value of persistence. This year one of her poems appears on the shortlist.

Only half a dozen poets overlap our first two volumes. And eight poets from Stephanie Bolster's longlist last year moved up to A.F. Moritz's shortlist this year. Taking both longlists into account, roughly only a quarter of the names overlap. This speaks more volumes than two Bests about Canadian poetry—and about personal ideas of excellence—it addresses publishing practices as well. Poets don't consistently publish in literary journals, so there's no guarantee each year that the best will be selected from the same pool. Obviously, ideas of excellence vary for each of our yearly guest editors. With only two volumes so far, we have published two very different constellations of poets. So, whose idea of excellence is it? Can there be two excellences, three, ten, a hundred? Our answer is Yes. Each year another guest editor does the daunting job of choosing the best and defining what best means—and narrowing that longlist down to the fifty poems that will be published in our yearly anthology.

In 2008 Stephanie Bolster carefully searched thirty-four magazines (print only) for poems to consider; in 2009 A.F. Moritz added twenty more (both print and online). We can't underestimate the vitality of the literary journals that publish the poems our guest editors select. If it weren't for the tireless editors of those magazines seeking out poems that they choose as the best for their issues, celebrating the established and unearthing new poets, then we couldn't do our . . . well, our best.

A.F. Moritz defines excellence in broad, juicy, philosophical terms in his introductory essay, positioning Canadian poetry on a world stage. For Moritz, what's finest about our poetry is that it holds its position internationally—in fact, it contributes to, challenges, and helps form a Canadian aesthetic that also makes an impact on the rest of the world. With its emphasis on the value of human connections and its insistence on the immeasurable weight of even the slenderest instances of love in the broadest sense, Canadian poetry joins a thriving world of poetry that values the dailiest of daily gestures as significant. These are poems that take as an underlying principle that what human beings really fight for—beyond oil, beyond territory, or even belief systems—are the almost mythically tiny and therefore most precious moments of personal peace. Such places of peace are also sites for the imagination. Is it too much of a stretch to say that as Canada plays its role as a world peacekeeper, so Canadian poetry plays its role in drawing our attention to the result of keeping peace: protecting the place of the imagination and its role in preserving the world?

How far is the reach of *The Best Canadian Poetry in English*? We were thrilled that our initial lively and comprehensive volume, so carefully edited by Stephanie Bolster (whom we cannot thank enough), found its way into classrooms, was tucked into bags for airline reading, has represented Canada both at home and abroad. This year we also launch in the US, and in coming years we hope to launch in the UK and in Mexico. (Tightrope is the only Canadian publisher with a Latina CEO.)

Many people put hours of hard work into this series, and foremost is Halli Villegas, the visionary who began Tightrope Books and whose energy makes it thrive. Editors Heather Wood and Shirarose Wilensky tirelessly handle the massive number of details and decisions that help complete each volume. The poets in our 2008 edition deserve another round of thanks and applause for all the readings across the country they have organized and all of the support they have given to our series. We thank David Bigham for his contributions to our efforts, Karen Correia Da Silva for the engaging look of our book, and Marilyn Biederman for sharing her rights knowledge with us. Thank you to the publishers who generously gave us permission to print poems that have been or will be published in collections. Dozens of journal editors have advised our process, and we are grateful to every one of them. Lastly we owe profound gratitude to A.F. Moritz for his acumen, time, and energy. You'll see just how he viewed this year's decision-making in his essay that follows.

Recently the British poet Michael Schmidt cited nineteenth-century poet Robert Southey in the *PN Review*. "The mediocres have long been a numerous and increasing race," Southey wrote in *Lives of Uneducated Poets* (1836), "and they must necessarily multiply with the progress of civilization." But at this moment in Canadian poetry it is the best poets who are multiplying—and rather than emblemizing a linear progress of civilization, they are investigating what it means to be civil in the widest, deepest sense. Canadian poetry is far better than good; it's better, even, than better. Here's our best for 2009.

Molly Peacock
TORONTO

Canadian Poetry Today

I.

The Feeling for Being: Canadian Poetry in a Landscape

Today's Canadian poetry is an adventure undertaken with brio. Its clarity and surge are evident equally whether its mood is dark or light, its pace meditative or militant. Great human hopes and debates are engaged with an openness that bespeaks humility, but with the confidence that leads an artist to firm outline, to vivid colour and movement. These qualities are evident on every page of *The Best Canadian Poetry in English 2009*. Let me choose these lines from Dave Margoshes's poem "Becoming a Writer":

> What could be easier than learning to write?
> Novels, poems, fables with and without morals,
> they're all within you, in the heart, the head,
> the bowel, the tip of the pen a diviner's rod.
> Reach inside and there they are . . .

An inspiriting invitation to each of us is created out of the "poem about poetry," which is often accused of being shop talk and the poet's self-centeredness. "Poetry must be made by all," Lautréamont famously said, and Margoshes's poem, like so many in this book, helps show us the poetry we all possess and make. I'm reminded of Emerson, with his idea of the poet as "representative person," important not for himself or herself but as the purest example of expression, which is the omnipresent impulse of human life and indeed of all existence. Something invisible expresses itself in each thing we see and touch. The mothering enigma (as the ancient Chinese put it) expresses itself in the ten thousand things of our world, whether we think of mountains and rivers, or of human occupations. The continual flow of poetry, the constant upsurge of poems, the presences within us that quietly but insistently press for a poetic burgeoning, are all ways in which poetry is both an emblem and an element of life's basic nature.

As the great Mexican poet, Octavio Paz, puts it, poetry is the "easiest thing, that which writes itself":

> The gush. A mouthful of health. A girl lying on her past.
> Wine, fire, guitar, tablecloth. A red plush wall in a village
> square. Cheers, glittering cavalry that enter the city, the
> people in flight: hymns! Eruption of white, green, fiery.
> The easiest thing, that which writes itself: poetry.[1]

Reach inside and there it all is, Margoshes's poem says to us. In fact, we know it isn't so easy to write a poem. To write a good one, worthy of the subject matter that lies within and around us, is hard and rare. Yet what Margoshes and Paz see is a deeper truth that accounts for the fascination of poetry: we are each a mirror and a container, and at times a voice, of the world as we've encountered it. When we feel the impulse of expression, this is the world, our world, coming to birth in a new form. We might recall what John Donne has told us about worlds: each of us "has one and is one." From this recognition springs the freshness that sweeps through the mind upon reading a simple poem, or all at once understanding something of a difficult one, in getting the idea for one, or working on it over hours, months, years, or at last finishing it properly. Our world has flowered. Its former brightness, without ceasing to be bright, is revealed to have been a rich darkness from which the world has now burst into further light.

Many things are mirrored and contained by the poems included here. Flip the pages and you see a collocation like Paz's of the vivacious elements of a moment of the world. Like Paz's yet different, entirely of our own places and times, from love-making on stream banks to being examined on a doctor's table, from the hieratic Buhler-Versatile 2360 tractor to a Canadian's moment in Hué in the presence of a maimed Vietnamese poet:

> Among layers of translucent palm leaves
> Thúy weaves her cosmos, weightless yet concrete.

1. Octavio Paz, *Early Poems 1935-1955*, tr. Muriel Rukeyser et al. (New York: New Directions, 1973), 79.

> Hours of sweat before she's satisfied
> and the poem is offered into sunlight
> revealing silhouettes of lovers lost,
> songbirds and a riverside pagoda,
> six lines of verse . . .

Cora Siré's poem of her visit to Thúy ("Before Leaving Hué") well expresses many aspects of the adventure of current Canadian poetry. It's a chosen journey into the unknown. For that reason, its every step is a new beginning and is accompanied by a trembling avidity, a mixture of lightsomeness and soberness, of reluctance and eager expectation. Everyone in the city tells Siré that she must visit Thúy. But the lyrical extension with which Siré describes her progress through the town silently reveals a certain reluctance, a fear to confront this poet, a resistance to the promptings Siré receives and to her own fascination. At last she does go to the war-ravaged poet. And she finds horrible damage and suffering, but transformed to creative joy: a person purged of bitterness and filled with poetry, a sight we at first feel we can barely endure to look at, which turns out to be the greatest gift and achievement, the most human triumph.

Each one of the poems included here gives a descent into reality and then a lift, an ascension of this sort: a release from the customary. Every one of them remembers at all times that the motive of the journey is to enlighten and to deepen our lives, the ones we have: a return to and an enrichment of the customary. This is one reason for the leaven of sobriety in the exhilarating approach to the unknown. A sort of dread is inevitable. Will what we encounter wreck our past or fulfill it, restore us to it or lead us away forever? What will be discovered? What new beings and what new knowledge will we encounter? "Reach inside and there they are," says Margoshes. This is not to say that we already possess everything, as if we are independent of the world and of experience, and can build a separate reality. It simply acknowledges that we cannot speak something until we do have it within us, the way we have whatever we were born with, plus whatever we encounter. Margoshes poem is not "subjective." It stands apart from the attitude that the mind constructs the world or colours it to such a degree that the original is not significant for us, or cannot be reached by us. Like all the poems in this anthology, it wrestles with this world-diminishing tendency, and refuses to submit.

The poems here defend faith and hope in human life and in the earth. They uphold the sense, primordial within us, that earthly life for all its hardships and problems is a good gift, the hope that human existence is not pointless, is not reducible to doings and distractions that for each of us end up six feet under. But on the other hand, our contemporary poetry most certainly does not preach, does not take up a message. On the contrary. What has happened is that the modern threats to hope, and to life itself, have simply revealed to poetry certain dimensions of its primordial and constant nature. In a situation such as ours today, these dimensions naturally tend to come to the fore, without poetry having to sacrifice any of its spontaneity, anarchy, and imaginative independence.[2] It protests, and evinces a truer way, simply by being what it is in and against the often thin, hateful cultural context it finds around it.

In the praise of life, Canadian poetry joins a broad international current originating in the Romantic movement, which in its contemporary form was probably first explicitly announced in the Spanish poet Jorge Guillén's *Cántico* (1927). It has been flowing broadly ever since. A poem entitled "Hope," written under the devastating siege of Warsaw in 1943 by the Polish poet Czeslaw Milosz, runs in part:

Hope is with you when you believe
That earth is not a dream but living flesh,
That sight, touch, and hearing do not lie.

2. Octavio Paz demonstrates and analyzes the mechanism by which poetry is an unchanging voice simultaneously ancient, prophetic, and present, while at the same time it adapts its outward form to circumstances such that it is also always "contemporary" in each historical context: Octavio Paz, *The Other Voice: Essays on Modern Poetry*, tr. Helen Lane (San Diego, New York, London: Harvest/HBJ Books, Harcourt Brace Jovanovich, Publishers, 1991), 143-60.

And in another poem, entitled "Faith," Milosz sings that "Even if you close your eyes and dream up things / The world will remain as it has always been / And the leaf will be carried by the waters of the river."[3] In holding this faith, or in some cases simply hoping for it, struggling against all the forces that now tend to destroy it, the Canadian poets collected here, whether they write about city or country, humankind or landscape, are nature poets in the sense given by one of them, Jan Zwicky, in a 2008 essay:

> the nature poet is not simply someone whose subject matter lies out of doors. The nature poet is, first and foremost, someone who does not doubt that the world is real—or, more precisely, someone who would resist the suggestion that the world is a human construct, a thing that depends on human speaking or knowing to exist.
>
> Well, who wouldn't? you might say. But . . . many . . . are persuaded by the thought, common since the seventeenth century, that mind-independent realities do not exist.[4]

Seemingly a heady intellectual matter, but it's intimately related to the question of respect for the earth in our personal, emotional lives and in our social, political lives. At stake is the preservation of both inner (psychological) and outer (natural, social, and built) environments that maintain vitality. At stake is a human city open to the mountains, the winds, the sky and the sea, not a lifeless enclosure.

Canadian poets constantly contradict, restrain and reverse the deathly tendencies of modern thought and behaviour through the

3. Czeslaw Milosz, *New and Collected Poems 1931-2001* (New York: HarperCollins Publishers, 2003), 49, 48.

4. Jan Zwicky, "Lyric Realism: Nature Poetry, Silence, and Ontology," *The Malahat Review* 165: *The Green Imagination*, ed. Jay Ruzesky and John Barton, 85.

resurrection—which also involves new impregnation, new birth—of truer, deeper elements of our tradition, and the importation of elements from other cultures. This is an international movement, as I've mentioned. Around the world it has been led by poetry, both as a voice speaking to this civilization of ours and as the living, prophetic example of a different possible way of seeing. In linking Canadian poetry to it, I've quoted Milosz and Paz. Here are some lines of Guillén's, to provide further connections:

> Through the air they float
> with a hovering murmur:
> many crossings and encounters
> of other voices, other existences.
>
> Least instance of adventure, smallest joy,
> who could uproot you from the fact
> of living? Of your being alive,
> still alive and death so near you.
>
> Right now, this, is the real. A riot.
> An uprising. A sour mixture.
> And the garden? Where is there
> any garden here? In the midst.[5]

The things the poet will bring from within are the actual ones encountered on this earth, subject to the fact—the dilemma if you will—that the poet, like each of us, can only possess them in his or her own ever-evolving way. This is one reason why it is important to receive the images, emotions and stories of all, since no one composes a human reality wholly and alone. My home town, my childhood, belongs to the many who shared them with me, and can't really be expressed by myself alone. To see our human world as fully as possible, we need as

5. Jorge Guillén, *Cántico: A Selection*, ed. by Norman Thomas di Giovanni (Boston, Toronto: Little, Brown and Company, 1965); text of "Jardín en medio" from this volume, 39-45; translation above by AFM.

many views as we can get. The antidote to subjectivity is dialogue, human togetherness. So Margoshes's poem reminds us that in fact we each harbour a world, and that we do tell its stories at least fragmentarily in our reverie and our conversation:

> Reach inside and there they are, the people
> one knows, their scandalous comments,
> the silly things they do, the unforgettable feeling
> of a wet eyelash on your burning cheek.

In the concrete way characteristic of Canadian poetry, Margoshes's poem vividly sketches in exactly what Guillén, in his symbolic language, conveys by "many crossings and encounters / of other voices, other existences." These people, their comments, the burning cheek, the wet eyelash, the momentary feeling of that, are examples of the "least instances of adventure," the "smallest joys": the details of this world.

This world with all its shortcomings. For "shortcomings" is what we can so easily see in this world when we compare it to heaven, to our personal hopes, even preferences, and to our technological dreams. People's scandalous talk and silly doings. A painful splinter. Rain that falls when it "shouldn't." All the way down to disease and man's inhumanity to man: existence as a riot, a perpetual uprising against us, a sour mixture. But the uprising is not always, and not only, against us. "Revuelta" is Guillén's word: returning, turning again, as in "revolt" but also as in "revolve" and "return." There is the constant return of things into the light, in always new forms. Maybe it suggests the question: Why should the world be easy? Why shouldn't its beings and moments barge and prick, making themselves felt by us, so often ready to demean or altogether ignore them? Requiring to be paid attention to.

This is what Zwicky argues for: "ontological attention." By this she means attention to the very being of things, of each thing and each moment. She goes on to say that this attention "is a response to particularity: this porch, this laundry basket, this day." Such attention itself, as well as the theory of it, is frequent in both the poems and the essays of Canadian poets now. For instance, the poet Tanis MacDonald comments, in a 2008 review of Tim Lilburn's book of poems, *Orphic Politics*, "The observing eye is the adoring eye" and finds in Lilburn's poems "a Hopkinsian 'haecceitas', the 'thisness' of attention that makes the physical world such a biding pleasure."[6] It is what the philosopher Gabriel Marcel termed "exigence for being" or "ontological need,"[7] a hunger and drive for being. Strange concept, for doesn't everything simply have being? Everything is, isn't it? Yes, but in us humans the connection to being can be interrupted, the feeling for it blunted. Or on the contrary, the feeling can be aroused, and the passion to be in contact with being can grow: we can cry out, like Tennyson, that it is "[m]ore life, and fuller, that I want."

The feeling for being not only can wax and then wane dangerously, come and darkly go. It does do so, in persons, civilizations, and epochs. It is not an automatic and steady possession. Canadian poets are strong among those heralding a desperately needed return to the feeling for being through love and engagement with the things that exist. And "love" is by no means a soft term here, lacking analytical thought's rigour (unless we mean its frequent rigor mortis). As Guillaume de Thierry put it, "Amor ipse intellectus est," love itself is intellect, love itself is understanding. In our sometimes splendid but sometimes difficult world, love is not always and simply love itself but is often the painful quest to love, and thus to understand, what is very hard to love and understand. Trying to understand how this world's "imperfection is the summit": words of the great French contemporary poet Yves Bonnefoy, and a theme that lovers of the English tradition will recognize as belonging to Robert Browning.

6. Tanis MacDonald, untitled review of Tim Lilburn's Orphic Politics (2008), *The Malahat Review* 165, ed. Ruzesky and Barton, 128.

7. For instance, in "On the Ontological Mystery" (1933) passim; reprinted in Gabriel Marcel, *The Philosophy of Existentialism*, tr. Manya Harari (Syracuse, N.Y.: Philosophical Library, The Citadel Press, 1956; 12th paperbound printing 1973), 9-46.

Among these Canadian poems from 2008 you'll abundantly find the attention Zwicky calls for, and which I've been calling love and the struggle to love. You'll find it bestowed, for example, on a child being dragged along by an adult, and on the man, too, who is doing the dragging; on a trip to an Ikea store seen as a journey to a contemporary sort of hell; on life as the devourer of its young at Pender Harbour, British Columbia, and on a waitress in a restaurant there; on people gorging themselves at a fashionable market and on the homeless person who haunts them; on dandelions; on the Yellow River in China; on the music of J. S. Bach. In other words, on the ten thousand things, ephemeral and mighty, painful and splendid. Some of the poems are concentrations upon a single thing (for instance, Shane Neilson's "Roadside Vegetable Stand") or a person (for instance, Matthew Tierney's "Nightingale"). Others are complex acts of attention that comprise many individual such acts; among these I might mention Anita Lahey's poem about a man tearing down a chimney, and Michael Johnson's opposite poem about steel making, its entire history caught in a visionary survey and seen as a human emblem. The poems Canadian poets are writing fulfill the variety that Zwicky recognized when she named among her examples of particularity both a laundry basket and a whole day.

II.

Visions of Balance: The Conversation of Canadian Poetry Now

The first poem here, Margaret Atwood's "Ice Palace," rejects and warns against the erection of private worlds of our own, with their inevitable inadequacy ("demiparadise / where all desires / are named and thus created, / and then almost satisfied") and with their ultimate deathliness. The second poem, the late Margaret Avison's "Two Whoms or I'm in Two Minds," takes an entirely different approach to the same issue. Avison's wit produces a poem slyly within yet against the tradition of poems in which two (or more) aspects of a person debate: soul and self, soul and body, the "resolved soul" and "created pleasure," "substance, shadow and spirit," "hic and ille," and the like. Avison starts thinking of the "all" that is within her, gathered in the experience of a long, attentive life. But immediately she finds out that she has to talk with each separate thing that makes up this all. The things have a selfhood, they are not simply hers to manipulate, to "think about." In fact, when she refers to them as "everything," they get mad at her. They demand dialogue. Each one has a voice, which mysteriously is quite its own, and not hers, even though it is she, the human being and poet, who must provide it. And what, or who, are these "all"?

> The barley-broom in long grass
> (hushed in its silken plumage),
> one or two beads picked off my
> childhood's dear fringed lampshade
> still bright, perhaps a
> vintage elm—that last
> evening, in good old summertime
> before the move out West (recalled
> regularly by my
> resolute father athirst for clear brook
> water babbling over stones all deep
> in blanketing snow).

The beloved minutiae of a life, almost intangible in their subtlety of persistence and interplay, in their bright darting or drifting through memory and imagination. Things that are, others that have been and now are gone, but remain in what they've given birth to in the world, in the life of a woman, in a poem. The substance of a life: experience with the grass, with the items and furniture of a house, with trees and streams, with one's parents, plus precious, never-completed, never-fulfilled glimpses of the parent's own relations to all such things. Pleasure, learning, loss of home, establishment of a new home, nostalgia, memory and praise of the dead. Man's rootedness and perpetual pilgrimage. The irreconcilable thirst for adventure and longing for security.

From that point the poem unfolds with the gracious, visionary balance characteristic of Avison. For her, no fashionable conclusion that we don't have a right to speak for other persons and things. But no simple speaking for them either. Witty sparring between the things that make up her life, on one hand, and her mind and poetry on the other hand, establishes the dignity and use of both parties: a balance between what she calls her territory, the realm of truths, and their territory, the realm of "particles." And so she can conclude:

> I like the word
> particulate. Its dictionary
> meaning has slipped my mind. But
> do let's have a cluster of
> particulates that I can
> dance among, with castanets.

> Peace be between and to
> us both!

A thought of mine, for which Avison would be a classic illustration, is that the greatest intensity lies in the most perfect balance of forces, which looks to the observer like a sort of repose, often referred to as harmony. And it is indeed a true "repose," a re-placing and re-positioning of our reality on a new footing. But it is tense with all power. It is the very opposite of the mere non-activity resulting from the absence of motivation or impinging forces. And it is also the very opposite of what is usually taken for intensity: a going to the extreme in one direction or another, which is in fact only a minor and distorted intensity, the development or release of one tendency while the others remain infantile.

The power of such balance, or the drama of the quest for it, or the longing or the suffering in its absence: these are essential contents of good poetry and are found throughout the anthology. So, thinking of an Edenic season, of being a young boy thirty years ago and working and roistering for a season with his idolized, open-hearted, devil-may-care older brother, Tim Bowling sings, in his poem "1972":

> And I loved without question a libertine Jesus
> cast in Caesar's bronze who listened all summer
> in days of uncut corn and nights oily

> with salmon runs to a song
> sung for an old man by a young . . .

The lines poise the hero against (and with) his worshipper, and Jesus against Caesar, the days against the nights, the corn of the fields against the fish of the waters and shores where the boys worked. "We were the future together," Bowling says, poising noun and verb against each other: were, future. And he presents the song that was the two brothers' anthem of that summer, "Harvest," in terms of an aching balance that recalls Yeats: "a man young and old." As he loops a tape so he can listen continuously to "Harvest," mourning and celebrating the moment it accompanied, he's led to a final prayer, or cry:

> New day,
> day, like all days,
> fated for loss,
> be more than an endless looping back,
> be a young shoulder in the sun,
> be heron-strike, the uncut corn,
> be the heretical act,
> be whaleback.

There's many a paradise (the word is from an old Persian word for garden) in a life, and many in a moment: "earth's recurring paradise," in Tennyson's phrase. And so are there many losses in a moment, many purgatories, many hells. In a 2008 essay, "Good as Green," the poet (and editor of the *Antigonish Review*) Peter Sanger quotes an aphorism by Franz Kafka: "The Expulsion from Paradise is eternal in its principal aspect: this makes it irrevocable, and our living in this world inevitable, but the eternal nature of the process has the effect that not only could we remain forever in Paradise, but that we are currently there whether we know it or not."[8] The struggle to know it, even when what we are confronting at the moment is a hellish fact, animates all the poems here, I believe. In Bowling's "1972" the horror is age and failure. Other poems confront other pain: social exclusions and definitions that can

8. Peter Sanger, "Good as Green," *The Malahat Review* 165, ed. Ruzesky and Barton, 78.

warp a life and mind, as in Connie Fife's and Sonnet L'Abbé's poems; the threat of illness in Barry Dempster's; the horrors of routine in Ken Babstock's poem and the equal horrors of the two-fisted freelance life in Carmine Starnino's. "You may be tortured or burned to steam," says Changming Yuan in his "Chinese Chimes: Nine Detours of the Yellow River," "but you will eventually find your impossible way / to the sea of blue sky." And there are also poems that start the other way around, that seem almost to start from heaven. But in them too the same effort and embrace will be found, the bringing of their joy to a darkness.

This effort and embrace are instinctive "theodicy," the justifying of God's (or existence's) ways to men. The hope, the never-abandoned attempt, perhaps the mere dream, to find that existence, with all its good and all its seemingly preponderant evil, is good. Zwicky puts it this way, in her "Practising Bach":

> Everywhere you look
> there's beauty, and it's rimed
> with death. If you find injustice
> you'll find humans, and this means
> that if you listen, you'll find love.
> The substance of the world is light,
> is water: here, clear
> even when it's dying: even when the dying
> seems unbearable, it runs.

Elsewhere in the poem she invokes a kind of music, which she finds in Bach, that goes beyond "even / the bright song of sex or hunger" in that it is "the unrung ringing that / supports" all other musics. Beauty and death are her terms in one passage, their equivalents sex and hunger are her terms in the other. Bach's music, she says in the next part of the poem, "speaks directly to, and of, life itself—the resonant ground of sex and death." She hears the music speaking like the light and water that are the "substance of the world." I'll refer one last time to the recent international tradition of poetry to which Canadian poetry contributes with vigour. In one of the great and seminal works of the twentieth century, Octavio Paz hungers for this same ground of being that exceeds and encompasses both life and death. In his long poem *Sunstone* (*Piedra de sol*, 1957), he prays to it as the mothering or generative darkness of origin, which was sensed by the ancient Mexicans as well as the ancient Chinese:

> hunger for being, oh death, our bread

>   life and death
> make a pact within you, lady of night,
> tower of clarity, queen of dawn,
> lunar virgin, mother of mother sea,
> body of the world, house of death

>   open
> your hand, lady of seeds that are days
> the day is immortal, it rises and grows,
> it has just been born, its birth never ends[9]

I've been speaking of one adventure of today's Canadian poetry but you will see as you read the poems of this anthology that its adventures are multiple. Many others could be picked out. And yet, a single window gives a perspective on the outdoors which, if limited, is whole. Again and again I'm struck by the way that each of these poems add something to the undertaking I've described. For instance, P. K. Page's "Coal and Roses: A Triple Glosa" recapitulates surprisingly the argument of Zwicky's essay that I quoted, "Lyric Realism." Page starts in the first poem of her triptych with frenetic pain at ecological destruction, an anguish that leaves the self ranting: the creative balance needed for poetry is nearly dissolved in desperation and hysteria, and the poem threatens to fly apart. The tone quiets and moves toward hope, or at least possibility, in the second poem:

> Perhaps the crocus, with its furry presence
> pushing toward the sunlight through the snow

---

9. Octavio Paz, *Piedra de sol / Sunstone*, English tr. Eliot Weinberger (New York: New Directions, 1991), 49, 51.

---

offers us hope that the whole world is waking
and making music.

By the third section, a transition through the earth of death and sex
has been made to a lower or a higher stratum, a thing that supports
all other existences, all other musics, a thing in which life and death
have made a pact with the result of perpetual beginnings, perpetual
dawns:

> There is a place, not here, not there. No dream
> nor opiate can conjure it—it is
> not heaven, though heavenly—it is its own
> element—not sea, not earth, not air...
>   It honours those
> who enter it like water, without wish
> vainglorious or trivial—a gift
> from realms of outer unimagined space . . .

The discovery of being is here, but so is the dialogue that keeps us
in the superior realm of things and persons that being serves. Page's
whole three-part poem, as a glosa, takes its departure from poems by
the great Russian twentieth-century poet Anna Akhmatova, and hence
has as its end not an intangible if most essential realm ("invisible
reality," as Juan Ramón Jiménez termed it) but a person, tribute to a
person, relationship to her, remembrance of her in the continuance
of her spirit. This dialogue with the past and the world is what I have
been indicating in part by placing Canadian poetry within the context
of contemporary world poetry and within the English tradition, just by
naming a few names, quoting a few lines: and so Page does by making
her poem a glosa, and so Zwicky does by writing her poem about Bach,
and by translating in her essay the poet Xiè Língyùn (fifth century CE,
Chinese) and quoting the poet Charles Wright (twenty-first century
CE, American).

This loving dialogue with the world and its ten thousand things,
especially its persons, is omnipresent in this anthology, and includes
honour and dialogue among the poets themselves. For instance, John
Reibetanz (whose poem here converses with the young Charles

Darwin) offered in a 2008 magazine a commentary on a widely known poem of Page's entitled "Planet Earth":

> Written by a woman who arrived on Planet Earth before most of the previous century (with its absence of dialogue between humanity and the rest of the planet), this poem stakes a claim for both international and environmental concord. As a glosa, "Planet Earth" engages in a cross-cultural dialogue with Pablo Neruda's "In Praise of Ironing," its source poem. Page takes Neruda's image— of poetry as a "pure white" remaking of the world—and opens it out like a freshly laundered sheet to demonstrate the "love" we all need to show in "smoothing the holy surfaces" of the planet itself. No eco-sermon, but an extended metaphor that delights and leaves us wiser.[10]

Reibetanz's "To Darwin in Chile, 1835" also employs an extended metaphor, reminding us of the impermanence of stone itself, the very face of the earth. In the 1830s the young Darwin was coming to realize this (at more or less the same moment that the poet Tennyson was writing, "The hills are shadows, and they flow / From form to form, and nothing stands"). So, Reibetanz says, it might seem that Peter, whose name means "rock," was just an impermanent, shifting human, like any of us: an unstable—in fact, a disappearing—basis on which to build a church, or anything. But by the same token, the poet comments to Darwin, there is something else in us, which we know in the image

> of another storm-tossed man whose feet
> tested earth's rocky sediment and found it seafoam,
> walking on water as you do now, as we all do.

Behind this rises Milton's tremendous and tender line from "Lycidas": "by the dear might of him that walked the waves." In walking this earth, the poem shows, we must and do balance the realities of permanence and impermanence: not to give way to the despair that the

---

10. John Reibetanz, in "Canada's Most Memorable Poems: The LRC Contributors' List," *Literary Review of Canada* 16.4, 17.

passing away of things can induce in us, but not to react by creating false, futile permanences, ice palaces. On the other hand, not to adopt the easy philosophy that all is change, but to admit and affirm that permanence—form and identity, the things and persons that we know and love—also represent a full half of reality.

It is a balance that M. Travis Lane's "The Confluence," which sits just about in the middle of this book, expresses beautifully. The restless poet wanders, dissatisfied with everything she sees on her walk, wanting it all to be either more permanent or, since it can't be permanent, then at least to be more rapid and fleeting, to be "ephemera, feathers." In this aggravated state of mind, she comes to a dull-looking bridge over the stream. On it, in the middle, sits a beggar, "who wished me blessings just halfway." "To sit all morning on this arc / of concrete!" she exclaims with an exasperated bewilderment that never leaves her. But in the middle of her mood there sits this beggar, "like the small bubble balancing / midway in a plumber's level / calm as the waters seemed to be, / bland, muscular, indifferent":

> Nothing seemed solid, nothing sealed,
> not even the graveyard markers or
> the new church growing within the old
> like a sapling on a felled log.
> Nothing was settled, not history,
> nor the rainbow bridge on which
> a beggar sat like a balancing.
> Whoever passed he blessed.

A.F. Moritz
TORONTO

The Best Canadian Poetry in English 2009

Ice Palace

Another ice palace. Another demiparadise
where all desires
are named and thus created,
and then almost satisfied. *Hotel*
might be an accurate label.

Not made of glass and marzipan
and steel, and jewel-toned water,
and opal gelatin that glows
like phosphorescent deep-sea fish, as
you might think at first. But no,

it's only dreams, it's only
clouds of breath formed into
words: the heavenly bed, the all-
you-can-eat breakfast. Invisible hands
bring food, smooth down

the sheets, turn on the lights,
cause violins to lullaby
the sugared air, clean out the wad of hair
you left in the porcelain shower,
and place a rose on your pillow

when you're not there. Where
is the fearful beast who runs the show
and longs for kisses?
Where are the bodies that were once
attached to all those hands?

Backstage it's always carnage.
Red petals on the floor.
You hope they're petals. Don't unlock
the one forbidden door,
the one inscribed
Staff Only. Do not look
in the last and smallest room, oh
dearest, do not look.

Two Whoms or I'm in Two Minds

Whenever I say, or even think:
all, launching out upon a
train of thought, then
such a clamour—
we're coming, we're about
ready, don't go without . . .
Without—whom?

The barley-broom in long grass
(hushed in its silken plumage),
one or two beads picked off my
childhood's dear fringed lampshade
still bright, perhaps a
vintage elm – that last
evening, in good old summertime
before the move out West (recalled
regularly by my
resolute father athirst for clear brook
water babbling over stones all deep
in blanketing snow).

How many are there
of you? Would it strike you as
better if I'd said,
"Whenever I think, or say,
everything . . ."?

—*thing*! What do *you* think?

All right then, that's
out, and the end
of *all* as well.

Now permit me to insist on
elaborating the thoughts I was
headed for . . .

You plan to do
that in
words?

      To
whom do I defer, now?

Words. Fancy,
for instance, saying that
Aplectrum hyemale (one of the
orchids) is the same as
Putty Root (its other name)!

Well, it *is* the
same plant.
Might we not both acknowledge
the borders? My
territory, the realm of truths, their
history, their
implications, and the
outworking in our ways.
             And yours
the fields of, what?
particles?

      I like the word
particulate. Its dictionary
meaning has slipped my mind. But
do let's have a cluster of
particulates that I can

dance among, with castanets.

Peace be between and to
us, both!

Autumn News from the Donkey Sanctuary

Cargo has let down
her hair a little and stopped pushing
Pliny the Elder on

the volunteer labour.
During summer it was all *Pliny the Elder,*
Pliny the Elder, Pliny

the— she'd cease only
for scotch thistle, stale Cheerios, or to reflect
flitty cabbage moths

back at themselves
from the wet river-stone of her good eye. Odin,
as you already know,

was birthed under
the yew tree back in May, and has made
friends with a crow

who perches between
his trumpet-lily ears like bad language he's not
meant to hear. His mother

Anu, the jennet with
soft hooves from Killaloe, is healthy and never
far from Loki or Odin.

The perimeter fence,
the ID chips like functional cysts slipped
under the skin, the *trompe*

l'oeil plough and furrowed
field, the UNHCR feed bag and visiting
hours. These things done

for stateless donkeys,
mules, and hinnies—done in love, in lieu of claims
to purpose or rights—

are done with your
generous help. In your names. Enjoy the photo.
Have a safe winter

outside the enclosure.

Flight

on this rooftop of 1000 parker street is a frozen lake
empty now
the ducks have flown south
and the geese are in victoria island, probably at the
butchart gardens
today january 16 2000
winter rains in vancouver have created a frozen lake
on the rooftop
outside my studio and my
memories follow you to the water's edge
watch as you test the water
my mind's eye etches
this provocative musical moment
into my soul my body anticipates
as it interprets your penetrating gaze
are you here or is it only my fantasy staring back
your invitation has flown away
I gaze at the gray frozen lake and remember
a flowing river and
I am transported
to a time where returning becomes at once impossible
I have walked with you forever
in the valleys of time and space
by the rivers of ever-flowing
where the sun melted
the icy rooftops of memory
watched as you poured the river
down your bodyscape
etching pathways
like rain on the window pane
making its way
slowly to the apex

the birds have taken flight
and nature has imprinted their image on
this frozen rooftop lake

1972

Harvest was playing. Shirtless,
the shade of Roman breastplate bronze,
my brother mended sockeye net.
Early August. With his hair down
below his shoulders, he looked like Jesus
helping John. Through the open window
of his sea-green 69 Mustang fastback
Harvest was playing. Over the mudflats
drifted the chloroform of ripening corn.
My brother's quickness bruised the meshes.
He corrected the past with needle-flicks
and sipped a second or a third Labatts.

Incomparable catcher of the curviest pitch,
dater of twins, master of blue eyes, bluer depths,
who could at will effect a gallant flirt
with an aged Greek widow and then sneak
off behind the Arms or Drake for a toke
with jumpy Yankees
newly fled from Nixon's unctuous yoke,
he believed in but a single cause: the open heart.

We were the future together. The air
that would give the heron's skull its turn
to shine in the sun washed over us.
I was still young enough to be accounted for
in niches in the framework of the kitchen door.
And I loved without question a libertine Jesus
cast in Caesar's bronze who listened all summer
in days of uncut corn and nights oily
with salmon runs to a song
sung for an old man by a young

who urged him to take a look at their lives.

Near and far as the autumn moon
that would rise suddenly behind
one of the delta's swaybacked barns
a whale's back broke the surface calm.
Gulls screamed. Blood flecked the sun.
My brother's shoulder roiled
in the snag and wash of time.

Three decades on,
Harvest is playing. I hit repeat
on the sixth track, think of calling
across the provinces to where Rome
has fallen, is falling.
Instead, I sip at
a second or a third Labatts.

New day,
day, like all days,
fated for loss,
be more than an endless looping back,
be a young shoulder in the sun,
be heron-strike, the uncut corn,
be the heretical act,
be whaleback.

Dante's Ikea

In the bedrooms of Ikea-land,
where love's theatres are assembled,
my sweetheart wept

upon the softest bed. I'd scoffed,
insisted I could neither rest nor play
upon these stock sarcophagi.

We shuffled over to Living Rooms
and sat on separate couches, neither one
prepared to pay unbeatable prices.

We drifted to kitchens, sharpened
knives, tested chopping blocks, drew
close, imagining winter-roasts and wine.

But the pepper-mills were plastic
and the wood was melamine.
We dared not taste the fruits.

With hearts in throat, we headed down
to the second circle. There, a horde
of howling children caged in glass.

Smiling wryly at my companion,
I queried why they balled their eyes out so.
And answering sombrely, she replied:

"They wail so because their parents
have lied to them again about the time.
Another eternity has passed them by!"

The toilets and the urinals hissed
just down the hall, but none emerging
came to claim these orphaned babes.

Feeling they ought to know,
I volunteered that mum and dad were lost
among the boxes down below.

At which they turned their red-eyed
demon-faces, and stoned my image
in the glass with hollow plastic balls.

From thence we proceeded till
we stood atop the stairwell to the final
warehouse floor, and there, we paused

and thus we prayed: "Dear God,
I hope the pieces fit this time."
Then down we tread

to the third, most dreaded circle;
and with each awful step,
we took the holy name.

The pillows brought no comfort.
The bathmats were all wrong.
The candles smelled like poison.

The vases lacked all grace of form.
The picture-frames and hangers,
though, were irresistible.

Further in, the daunting stacks
of all that we'd been shown above.
The boneyard of domesticity,

where bits and pieces of living
lie in boxes like the dead.
Billies, Nannas, Ivars and Johans

stacked on scrap-wood pallets.
What if Robin's legs and Markor's screws
were mixed with Mikael's top?

"Dare we crack it open?
Look inside? Is it gauche
to show a lack of faith down here?"

"I don't care," she answered,
"nothing matters any more." It seemed
we'd found the fabled vale of despair.

And just beyond, awash with sun!
—O blessed sun!—Hope.
You are meant to see the light

and stand within a few short metres
of that happy plain we call the parking lot.
With eyes asquint, you can spot

your car. But by Zeno's law, the line
you're in is an infinite series of half-steps,
halves of half-steps, halves of those.

A twisting child, red and raw with sobbing,
entangled in a wire cart-seat, shrieked
and blew green bubbles from her nose.

At the checkout, we surrendered our identities,
signed our names away; then wheeled off,
beyond the glaring exit-doors.

Even now

Even now when muscles slacken and bones thin out
—and why do they, if not to let in light—the body opens

to cordial air, the courtesy of trees, fork-tailed swallows
in flight, their joints and ligaments ours. Atavistic us.

In early angel state, eye and ear migrate. They're at our elbow.
Down on our knees. The world's infolded in every limb.

In September's stirabout, what was enough, is not enough:
Frost at night and summertime by day, the air is appetite.

The stipple tongue's all over taste. The lucent skin is lavish.

Turns out that old adage about angels on a pin
refers to the body: How the five jig and sing in every cell.

Up out of the years' sleep, the body divines dispersal.
What's next is near, and already we are here in afterthought.

Space Is a Temporal Concept

The snails mount the stairs up the left side
   of the temple followed by treble notes, a cappella,
loud as a jazzed-up car with its bass vibrating
   our ear drums, and suspended overhead
is a two-ton Aztec calendar or its facsimile.
   I'd like to point out the velveteen texture of the
golf greens, dependent on enough herbicides and fertilizer
   to poison all our drinking water forever.
In the centre the Wide-Eared Clown and Lord Death
   stand back-to-back on a simple stage, locked in
sardonic debate, while a roulette wheel spins, elevating
   the diorama up onto another level of existence,
for which, dear Diana, not even your spectacular
   marble profile at the Met has prepared us. Now,
two archways rub shoulders, a crane lifts
   wheat and barley fields, multiple heirloom varieties
of hydroponics tomatoes, and every object
   shimmers, images etched across ever more luscious
faces and tender lips. Before our thoughts were formed
   they were being broadcast from the diamond-shaped mobiles
in a fever of daylight, but delicately, because time, evil in intent,
   is zipping by. They put your left foot in butter and then
your right foot in and as the vision recedes, the pastry chef
   is crowned and rides off on a float down Fifth.
The arrow says up, we follow doggedly because
   all the water's been transported in metal pipes
and aqueducts, everyone who makes it to the top is rewarded
   with fountains of clean, aerated H_2O, the children are
offered ice cream, free of course, and we gorge on marshmallows,
   gather around fires that spring up spontaneously
as far as the eye can see. When we begin the long migration
   toward magnetic north, the homeless are with us, we can see

underfoot the fault lines, deep and ragged, the absent
    loved ones join us, my father included, and all the emotional
debris of a lifetime hovers overhead in a vast vertical column,
    flashing and rotating, as eager to befriend us as a lost puppy.

Mercy

The old god drops his flesh and bones
and rushes down as wind and nothing else,
not word or light or mercy. It batters the town,
slams a sheet of plywood against the curling rink,
shoves me down the alley in my slippery shoes.
In the third yard down, on a metal clothesline pole,
strung by their necks with ropes, two coyotes sway,
weight and counterweight in a faceless clock.
Beauty graces them, even now, death graces them.
Is it a curse to love the world too much,
to praise its paws and hooves,
its thick-furred creatures, each life a fear in me?
The wind saves nothing on this earth.
The coyotes hang like coyotes from an ugly tree.
Their throats don't make a sound.

Groin

Drop your drawers, doctor-talk, making me
feel like a dresser stuffed with wrinkled shirts
and clumps of socks. Inhuman to be
naked here, Calvin Kleins twisted around my ankles.
An X-rated cartoon, a bare-assed platypus.
Turns out I'm also swollen lymph glands,
a groin bulging with the need for attention.
It all started with an infected tooth, but that's
not important as I stretch out on the table
like luncheon meat. I'm breeze where breeze
rarely goes, new hands lifting and squeezing,
fingers joined together in a tiny oh. I'm a startled
glow, a testicle pearling with fluorescent light,
surrendering its eggy code of secrecy.
Beyond dirty thoughts, further out than
erections can reach, a strange tenderness
softly prickles, pores exhaling, saggy and sallow
smoothing their entanglements. This *is* human
after all, a scrutiny that only love can muster:
              the desire to really know.
I lie there, held, seen, wondered, as we talk
about the marvels and mishaps I've always been.

Bite Down Little Whisper

the sky cradles an absent blood   silence of washed
veins through the trees   bloodlines flushed out
                                        and carried away

hematic glyphs written once in the air and erased

we are stained by the invisible in the lowering day
by the arterial blush of the world   meanwhile
the ghosts of our fallen hair rise up to heaven
our shed skin follows us through room after room

meanwhile our thin eyelids open and close
our home disappears   and reappears
as the sum of our vacant ontology

pale ache beneath our tongues   pale metaphysics

The land that is nowhere, that is our true home
to use Chang Po-tuan's words as talismans
shining syllables to hang in the branches
for luck   for chimes when the wind returns.

*

late hours among the weeds   grass top heavy
with exoskeletons   film noir and animal weights

cats beginning to head out across fields
dusk banked up against their fur like dark birds

a maggot with a gondola's long shine over water
skimming the surface of a mouse lying in the brome

a doe standing still in the acquittal of light
each leg holding a presolar energy
                    and a mouthful of air

and we're there most days as witnesses
pressing our headaches against windowpanes
watching and waiting for time to gather us in
waiting for strange brushstrokes across our hearts

our hands just out of reach   our sight laid low
                                    in the guise

death filling in the blanks as holy writ and a steady grace
nothing profane   microorganisms written
as sacred text on the painted tissue of things as they curl
as they die and are assimilated   curl and fall.

*

the end of day is a tapestry of one thread
laid flat across the landscape a thin string
pulling sparrows up and over black hills

evening comes   dharma of bruised lips
blowing out the candles   loosening light
and time around the heart

so that night is a brief hurt among the illuminations
and sleep is an anatomy lesson without a body.

*

midnight or thereabouts   clouds gathering
like pressed flowers in a weightless book

a few stars on black paper   a few missing

among spruce trees I've built a small life
a temporary narrative   Ogam cuts in solitude
my fire swaying   colouring outside the lines

night's drift carrying the shine away

a night with a bad tooth in its jaw
the ache snug between the ferns
a whisper of pain   telegenic among
hawk's beard and groundsel

among intercessions of the vetchling

there is no metaphor for such infliction
so bite down little whisper   black incisor
right there where the inaccessible meets silence
where yesterday's words draw the light in

bite down and sit tight   just there
where my fingers look for solitude
in the landscape   along mossy
stitches in the wood   along jinx
and orifice   dung and honey
where our shudders first ruptured
                        into language
language into deeper sleep.

*

camo of deep woods   black and grey
double dyed on quietude   tincted
with shadows of coyotes blading by
eviscerators flat against the breeze

hunter and hunted bloodied   processional
Vedic lip-sync of teeth on flesh
*If the slayer think that he slays, and the slain
think that he is slain, neither knows the
ways of truth*

so bite down little whisper   right there
where we live layered between form
                                          and formlessness

where the Katha Upanishad's songs
are like bedclothes laid on the living
and the dead . . . *neither knows
the ways of truth*   I kneel to this
every time   without knowing why

on nights like this it gives me comfort

on nights when I would rather
be a rabbit orbiting a celestial hunger
lost in the clover's gravitational pull

or one of those crows high in the branches
above me   just out of God's reach
splinters of sleep passing through their bodies
each feather trembling in its separate dream
each shiver holding twelve skies.

*

I tend my fire   a little lip at flame's end
a little curl of speech turned to smoke and ash
something redemptive in the burning wood
almost spoken of in the moment   almost heard

moon rising   white cathedral where we all
eventually go to pray   our only church
when we try to hush the dog and hush the rose
listening for improvisations of the one silence
one emptiness   ear to stone

I tend my fire   a little galaxy at flame's end
a little curl of sidereal time turned to smoke and ash
burning dry sticks and branches   a reclusive
iconography   melancholia and its sacrament
                              drear and aura

drowse of the absolute somewhere above me
cloistered and nodding off among microbes
among changelings and starvelings
incessantly drifting   little fadeaways
on their deep journeys through the virga

seated beneath the overhang of spruce boughs
my grief and ignorance want for nothing
feed off an absence   autolytic and bittersweet
feed off a synaptic loss   that space between
two words   where our souls will finally
              be tonsured and nail-clipped
our hearts sewn shut over our eyes

tonight I bow my head   tonight the darkness
bows back at me from its shining abyss

meanwhile a chrysalis retools its enzymes

meanwhile grasses grow along the deer path
each a copy of a beautiful mother.

Babies' Cottage

Where do we come from?
What are we?
Where are we going?
Don't ask.

The mountains across the harbour
were a chain of offshore islands
before their long slow crash
into British Columbia.

The ground we walk on, hard-packed clay and gravel,
was carried down the mountains
by glaciers and rivers now vanished.
The hospice around the corner

once housed family court;
before that it was Babies' Cottage, an orphanage.
Someone sits by a lamp in the fog-shrouded lounge.
Above the fog, we are told, the sun is shining.

Six Times

How long will you mope among the zinnias
On your grave, sitting crosslegged in the dirt

Gazing and brooding
Running soil through the jointed flue of your hand?

Six times I stood upon a shoulder-smooth hill
And called your name

But you shook your head only
As though at the landing of a thing

And brushed the small weight of my voice from your listening.

Little "o" Ode

Feeling unfit to undo the thong
of the *Fifth Symphony*'s sandal,
unwilling to make a bust of the famed bust
with a blunt coal chisel of verse,
and utterly incommensurate to parting
that commanding shock of hair
with a comb of flimsy lines,
I panegyrise instead the bite marks
on the dowel* that transmitted his piano's
vibrations to his deafened skull,
allowing him to snatch the *Ninth*
from the grasp of eternal silence.

I hold the teeth marks up to the light;
they are deep and decidedly Romantic:
proof of his bulldog grip on glory.
To fall into an incisor's divot is to
plunge into a bottomless ravine from
the highest Bavarian summit—
deeper yet, into the frown-furrow in his brow.

He once parted the vapours of demureness
and mediocrity with this humble Excalibur,
but to take the dowel in hand today
is to raise a frail abandoned chrysalis
after the swell and profusion
of summer wings has come and gone.

*Beethoven used a dowel to transmit the musical vibrations of his piano to his skull,
allowing him to play and compose long after he was certifiably deaf.

A New World Poem

1

I am surrounded by the familiarity of old friends
in their home made of beadwork, dogs, fresh coffee,
missing the Fraser, her canyons and fierce rapids.
My longing for you swallowed me in my dreams,
bridges raced across my thoughts.
Johnsons, your land was where you stood
and my son spoke freedom out loud,
a new word on his palette.
The place where fears fled downstream,
treading water before being pulled under.
Eagle overhead, companion and vigilant.
A moment of poetry painted upon cement piercing the river.
A bridge named after a wealthy rancher occupying stolen land,
sacred site and burial grounds.
Some surfaced, others still in hiding.
From the streets of Vancouver the river is no longer distant.
In between streaking cars its waters run freely now.
My home far away, a constant presence under my skin.

2

My hair is longer now, more white streams running.
Still, I am told, I look younger.
Less tension around my eyes,
Less disillusionment pulsing through my veins.
Cynicism by my side.
The reckoning that arrives with the forties.
No longer hesitant at the sight of myself,
in stride with the season.
Not afraid to die
or live
or love

or grieve
or laugh
or run through tall grasses
or dive into freezing waters
or fall in love
or write of falling in love.
Not afraid
to love
myself,
another,
poetry, flesh, imagination,
dreams or
my outrage.
In love with each
of my joys and tribulations.

3
these days iron deposits slither out of goliath boulders making
shortcuts from crevice overhang. I have become
the last precipice they teeter on, my flesh falls away, our
bones crash, bruised by stone, thrown, always under the
threat of death by drowning, pardoned repeatedly.
I keep track of good fortune.

4
By whose gaze do I name myself?
How do I translate the many movements that have shaped
me?

5
I cannot say I love women more than men.
I can say I sing praises often for other women.
I can announce my love of anyone who is unafraid
to be themselves, to allow their landscape to change.

I cannot deny another the ceremony of a poem,
though some words I have kept hidden from exposure.
I cannot claim to be more than I am,
my insides lined with story and love.

6
Went DownTown to the Eastside
dead junkies dangled from streetlights.
Christmas decorations hung by the City of Vancouver
others being raised at the last minute.

7
the mirrors I faced
never offered the same reflection twice
nor has my outrage turned to hatred

8
A bridge led me to you,
from salt water to autumn streams
bleeding into the Fraser.
Another leads me back to the minerals
in your blood, twisting and churning their way
into my heart. Warmth against any cold front or blizzard
blown across by memories from Saskatchewan.
A bridge leads me home.

9
I have a vision:
there will come a day
when we will sing praises
instead of lamentations.

10
I got caught stealing

popsicles
by hiding them
in my socks.
It
was
the
dead of a whitened
winter in Saskatchewan.
In
The 60's.

11
A day when no one human being's
heart is broken by the   single
word   no
a day when simple truths
no longer die so far away from home
on streets
instead of
cool damp earth.

12
I dreamt of a council of women.
Their voices are drowning
out the noise of whirling army helicopter blades.
Watching soldiers, watching me.
Eyeing each other through binoculars.
I sit against a mountain face.
Annie Mae Aquash, Helen Betty Osborne
and Oka are still
on my mind.
Another summer of
discontent behind us.

13
I can say
I have been named
princess, squaw, halfbreed,
manhater, bulldyke and savage.
I can say that through my own gaze
I am
I am.

14
cree
    daughter
    mother
    lover
    friend
    lesbian &
    many spirits,
    ally to many
    men.
one day
    a grandmother
    woman

15
The vines have wrapped their fingers around the old maple.
I glimpsed the purple, mauve fuchsias of last summer.
A new highrise is about to block the view.
Glad I moved. Soon there will only be good memories.

16
Q: are you still writing?
A: yes.

17
I cannot claim to love a tree more than this sheet of paper.
I cannot announce myself to be more than I am.

18
I dreamt I had goat hooves, hollow horns, coarse hair,
and scaled the face of a rock slide.
Reached new forest and sage brush.
From far below
women are watching me.
I can see them, smoke and river
                    beauty
                    smoke
                    river.
I can see women around the fire
beside the river.

19
My backpack is heavy again.
Years of carrying pounds of paper.
My age.
Tried a laptop. Tried.
Journals getting thinner,
I can carry more of them this way.
Drafting my way through the maze.

20
Q: do you still write poetry?
A: yes, poems for a new world.

Pender Harbour

A dream among the firs and hills, among
the boats that toss upon the waves forever
leaving and returning: I an imprisoned witness
to the crone's ritual, her slow separation
of life from bodies. Every night she gives birth—
 blueprints of limb and nerve in wooden likeness
of her labour. This time her soothing hum
peels a boy's skin, enchantment of all
that lies beneath: the warring parasites
that churn the stomach, pus and bile, bone
(the body's only firmness) made slack
by privation of meat for muscle, blood
running thick to infuse it all—blood,
symbol of life and dying both. Tell me,
child, does her song bring you pleasure?
Each time I woke I felt sick, fell
into sleep to watch some other alternation
of her work until, finally, I wondered:
what kind of mind conceives such things?

And chained to char, to blackened pew, returned
in shackle to her darkroom undeveloped, I asked
why she did it, slow bleeding of the son,
until the shell alone remains. Mirthless
laughter:

> would you be Dante or Milton
> and observe no horror? I want only body,
> perpetual movement in accepted form, this simpering
> lung returning air the moment it is full,
> before, even; the always emptying bowel,
> never satisfied, lest the restless brain

find time to think. I am the first machine.
You are nothing.

So, earth. I woke up. The canary trucks lumbering
outside tend to death, are dead, but not
the white breath driving them. In Madeira Park
they claw out another space for real estate,
for little shops to sell cups and plates
to Americans grazing free from their native fields,
the grid of their farms like simple math, the towers
that issue summons and random directives
cemented into law. The logging and fishing,
are these not life? To dig for a building? Or
the repetition of the girl's movement
from home to café, constructing sandwiches
like breathing, like filling and emptying.
Think of her now, make that girl real:

Could I sit, and look upon you now?
Say who you have been. Your hair I can
never touch, so dark, soil-brown,
pools in shoulder cleft and tends,
like a labourer's, to anarchy. And so
the ones who serve most fully: no time
for hair or fine clothing. Sweat upon
your lip and brow, hurry, a downward
turn of mouth, anger, threat of eviction:
you'll have to work longer. Forearm
slanted lady-like above your waist,
wrist limp, until the man you love
arrives. He'll fix the pick-up after work.
Then, sandwich-maker, you flared,
words a knife's edge to cut not spread.
I recalled an hour before, your voice

rising at the end of every line,
it made me think you were serving me,
were nothing. I was wrong: you're the centre,
no coffee-girl here. Hope you make
your birthday dinner, hope the guy's
not covered in grease, sitting at the Hopper.

Oh mad dream of life,
underground man, that knows no satisfying,
even when it wanted truly to die, and so to live!

Home Movies, 8 mm

What holds you here, besides small shocks
of delight, then embarrassment, seeing these too-fast
films unravelling, mute but for the sprockets'
plastic chatter, an outboard roar as the almost-

antique projector, Yashica 1965, splashes clips
of faces in their once-loved form (forgotten
till now—interred in the nerves) on screen. What keeps
you here tensed, if not frustration

at your impotence to intervene—reach back
and brace the hand holding the camera that pans
away, again, with a young hand's
impatience to contain all: slaphammer first home, a block

of Main Street rising between houses
to a mine's brontosaur headframe, in the laser-
blue noon of subarctic winter—
then, in a dress-coat the colour of roses,

a mother, breaking the frame, waving a newsreel's
sped-up wave, while from the left a dog lollops in,
unrecalled as ever so small,
so awkward!—and you rush the screen,

kneel closer and again the camera
swivels away—
stout neighbour in dark overcoat and fedora,
mouth going—while to the left you can almost *see*

her and that dog in the dark, or wherever the place
is, forty years out of frame (both dead now), as the man in the coat
tips his hat and the scene cuts, to white. Greece
then, Nipissing, faces in flashes, the light

sallowed, even children stained by that ambery
tone, as the lens pivots faster, refuses
focus, close-up—the patient frame. I know how memory,
what these reels were meant to fortress,

aims the same fickle lens, leaving gaps, apertures
in the record, but what of the eye itself, as it glides
over a lifetime's loves the same way, careless
and rushed, a manic amateur,

and the little reel clicks down inside?

If I could start over, I would stare and stare.

The Church of Steel

Lathe, knurl, taper, thread: steel is god.
Oilsheened, bladeburnt by the kerf
of the tool's carbide tooth, see how
the excess molts, how the shavings rope
and wobble: the turned thing itself turned
bewitching. Shavings have scissored
my palms, worked straight through
my hands, made my skin a bloody bloom.
Yet I return to steel and emery cloth,
to lathed aluminum like razor lace,
to rust dust and drills and dies.
I play precision: hone, sink, buff, bore,
to see the coils sizzle and spin, knowing
my mastery is fleeting, and the cost—
these scars—simply offerings
to a god whose face I form.

Love Amid the Angloculture

Is it not of the same gravity
as going to war,
the decision to love?
The opening of the gate like the cell
allowing a change in its membrane
to a porousness, allowing the free flow
of connection between seas
of our unconsciousnesses.

Yes, I will
open the underground channel:
Your water flows into my water.
Have you kept your water clean?

The surfaces opening onto my hollows
the walls of intestine, the acidic
flesh of stomach, the tender bronchiules
of my lungs, soil:

all of it, soil, rained on
by my drink and planted with nutrients,
proteins, precious metals, seeping
into the red earth of me

oh and my insides heaved by storms
there was a quake
when I learned my language said
my skin meant "less human"

a fissure opened:
a man-made blast disrupting the natural
tributaries of sense, sensation, good sense:

The root of my happiness
was pulled up by the fronts
meeting against one another
as my mind tried to school myself
to be precious amid unconsciousness

fear pushed like a fat bulb
into the loam of my gut
the word they made of their fear
and shoved down my throat
is now inside-me
no matter how I shit and shit and vomit

I have digested the radioactive walls
of national ego:
my pride ever has the tincture
of meeting you as the humiliator, love

it has taken a few short
thirty five years
to know I am all time

to know what our ancestors mistook
when English put the word
whiteness around the finesse.

Man Tearing Down a Chimney

1.

He wheels his pick-up into the drive,
munching gravel, casting a wake of white
dust. The gears rev taking the hill,
and the metal bars and crossbars that will

rise into staging, a giant Meccano set, thunk
and roll, banging and clanging the trunk
in which happy retrievers have stood,
ears blown back, in which sheets of plywood

have lain next to big black toolboxes,
been shoved aside by cardboard boxes,
been stained by ducks shot down, their blood
forming runnels all the way home from the gut.

It's not his way to sneak up on it.
He won't kick or taunt or insult it.
The clanging and revving and crunching
serve as warning to the rotting, mulching

brick, the hard-baked brick, the flaking,
cracking, chipping, weakening brick taking
hold of the house like a battered hero
clung to a cliff wall, praying he'll see tomorrow.

2.

The chimney and the man have both reached
their thirties, but he is limber, lithe. Each day he better fits his torso;
his arms and legs
become like tools, gleaming—they beg

to be used fully, without restraint, and in
moments such as this, when an ending
must be ushered in before it collapses
onto a child, a dog, a car, or crashes

through the roof. The red tower of clay
still pleases the eye, dividing the house, the sky
beyond the roof peak, the shoreline's call
through spruce, pines, marshes and the pall

that gathers wet and grey over the ocean
on troubled mornings, like dismal notions
swept from Hades' crowded rooms—
But trees and fog don't matter, nor upon whom

the fault lies for its half-blocked flue,
its shoddiness that always meant even two
days of wood smoke might set it ablaze.
The facts: it leaks, and must be razed.

3.

Hammer in hand, the man climbs. The sun
watches, as do bulky clouds that threaten
to open, as does the woman on the ground
who thinks, without warning, of their drowned

great-uncle. He lies—Does he really? Did he
wash up? Was he pulled?—in the cemetery
down the shore, due east of this new violence.
He might have lived to thirty, too. Had the sense

to begin, as his nephew does, with the soft rot,
the south-facing sections that are so shot
they need only be tapped to disintegrate
and cascade like handfuls of soil straight

back to earth, where all dead things land.
But first, a moment when both stand
together. The man leans forward to whisper,
or to listen for old fire vapours

in the flue (like watery songs in seashells),
or simply to establish his footing on the shingles.
Bells, she calls for bells, as arm and hammer
swing. O brick, O uncle, O clamour.

4.

Descending a mountain can be more trouble
than scrambling up. Turning a built thing to rubble
is also a battle with gravity, against habit
and persistence. Try convincing a pair to split

though their union, once alchemic, no longer makes
sense. This clay and concrete have three decades
of weather and smoke between them, of stillness
and height. And so, a boot is required to wrest

some pieces from the core. A phone call
must be made for the delivery of a maul.
Hours pass and clouds thicken and the man
now stands wide-legged on a plank,

five or six feet up. It sags. Winds rise. Sweat
streaks his arms and neck. It's a safe bet
black flies fill his ears. But the top of the chimney
lies ruined below him, a landslide of debris.

In the gable, a gaping. Along the seam, ants,
the dampness they desire. In his hands
the long handle to the black weight he aims
at the most resistant brick. He gives it names,

too, this motherfucking brick, but under
his breath (the woman doesn't hear).
She gapes like the exposed gable as the maul
arcs up and in. Behind the brick, the wall

fronting the living room quakes as though
the gods were launching tremors from below.
He twists and heaves, tearing through space,
a dancer, believer, every ounce swung, no waste.

5.

They sit in the kitchen, a bottle each, solemn.
Every brick and chunk of brick has fallen.
A blue tarp blankets the gable hole and thin wall,
and just in time, too: rain runs down it, and all

her thoughts run alike: Here's a man who
broke a chimney's back because he knew
where to hit and how hard. But no. I think
his secret was merely to start, and at the brink

of defeat, hit harder. Like a woman who's just
given birth, he has earned silence. Thus,
she quells her wonder. They tip their brown glasses.
His day, in dust and shards, blankets the weeds and grasses.

The Confluence

A milky brown, the rivers slid
below the greying cottonwoods
like great pale snakes. I found them dull.
The bridge from which I looked at them
seemed nothing much. A beggar
wished me blessings just halfway.
Early, I thought, and chilly.

To sit all morning on this arc
of concrete! That man seemed
like the small bubble balancing
midway in a plumber's level,
calm as the waters seemed to be,
bland, muscular, indifferent.

On the other side the written past
stirred mildly in the grasses,
not quite washed over, settled. The carved stones
seemed wrong. I wanted wood, ephemera,
feathers and cloth. I wanted leaves
that as I watched them faded brown
and then into the silky grey
of water, weather, passing time.

Light flickered as if the rivers stirred
the shadows, clouds, the sanded paths.
Nothing seemed solid, nothing sealed,
not even the graveyard markers or
the new church growing within the old
like a sapling on a felled nurse log.
Nothing was settled, not history,
nor the rainbow bridge on which

a beggar sat like a balancing.

Whoever passed he blessed.

The Night Market

In the night market, a woman with filthy hair
and clothes dripping with threads
stares at the vats of curried fish balls
and braised tripe as if at a storefront window
in Beverly Hills, her face squeezed by hunger.
Around her, hordes of families and couples,
lips shining with grease, reach for the next reward—
even the teenage girls on diets
pinch skewers of quail or scallop
between manicured nails.
I wish I could feed this stranger
like the baby seagull we found one day
in the bushes by the water, so docile or damaged
it let us put our hands on its body, suffering our touch
with eyes bland as beads
in exchange for a morsel. I could buy her
a meal and not miss it. Instead
we gorge on dumplings and waffles,
the starch sloshing in my stomach
like wet cement as the crowd roars past,
goldfish mouths flapping, the sky raining down
bitter black ash, soot in my nose and throat
from the cooking fires. This is the Richmond Night Market
on a Saturday night, our stomachs straining our waistbands,
bodies bathed in smoke and spices,
the sunset a tanker explosion
spilling across an oil-soaked sea. I stuff shrimp gyoza,
squid tentacles, kimchi pancakes
into my mouth as if into someone starving,
someone I'm trying to save.

Actaeon

"Be still now: listen."
—"Siren," Fiona Ann Papps

I was not hunting that day. I only drew blood
when other young men, teeth crowding their
smiles, shamed me away from the clay my hands kept

shaping into flawless imperfections of the woman
those quivering trees in my dreams were embracing.
I was fleeing my father, my friends' fathers, the season's old

wine loosening talk of stalking one beautiful woman after
another as they strolled through the courtyard, dropping
them to their knees with thick supple arrows, bleeding

their cries, watching their eyes roll back under lids, and before
their beauty could recoil, trap and destroy them, leaving seed
so deep it would sprout rhododendrons that drip mad honey.

Walking for hours, I lost myself in ripe green light
of cypresses, and thought they whispered "Go back
to the safety of oaks, goodness of olives, airy seductions of myrtle trees."

But I had found my dream, and a glade, and pond rippling
through my veins as I approached. And saw her, bathing, her moon
face pregnant with sun, torches for hair, a bear pendant

around her neck, and breasts that split my vision open
like a pomegranate, staining red my eyes as they reached out
to know her. She glanced at a quiver of silver arrows nearby

and stars circling her head grew brighter, so she moved
toward me, emerged, skin shedding moonstones and pearls.
Drew an arrow, strung it, aimed at my heart, and pulled.

Then laughed. Lowered her bow. It is true. The antlers and hoofs.
In my sudden brown hide, I stood unafraid, as she rubbed aloe
where the arrow grazed my flank. She draped her hair

over my antlers and they were on fire but I still did not fear.
Not when her hand, a crescent moon, slid into my breast
and I was again human. White light seared my heart. She took

my hand between her legs, and there was blood. Not a virgin's,
she said, but your kind won't believe if you tell them. Do you want
me, now? Yes or no, either way I will spare you.

I tell you this from a rocky island cave where the priests
won't find me. Where my father won't choke me with incense
and poison me with more lies. Where my friends won't insist

that the scar on my chest was from wrestling a wild boar
or a jealous Thracian whore. Or self-inflicted in my madness.
That the stains on my thighs are birthmarks, and always there.

Becoming a Writer

What could be easier than learning to write?
Novels, poems, fables with and without morals,
they're all within you, in the heart, the head,
the bowel, the tip of the pen a diviner's rod.
Reach inside and there they are, the people
one knows, their scandalous comments,
the silly things they do, the unforgettable feeling
of a wet eyelash on your burning cheek.
This moment, that, an eruption of violence,
a glancing away, the grandest of entrances,
the telling gesture, the banal and the beautiful,
all conspire with feeling and passion to transport,
to deliver, to inspire. Story emerges
from this cocoon, a crystalline moment, epiphanies
flashing like lightbulbs above the heads
of cartoon characters. All this within you
where you least expect it, not so much in the head
as under the arms, glistening with sweat, stinking
with the knowledge of the body, the writer
neither practitioner nor artisan but miner, digging
within himself for riches unimagined, for salt.

Song for the Song of the Sandhill Crane

It eschews the ear,
with its toolshed, its lab, its Centre for Advanced
Studies in Hermeneutics and Gossip,
to boom exactly in my thorax,
rattling the bones and waking the baby. Garroo:
the o's are caves of lunar gravity, the rolled r
recalls the ratchet of life and death.
Why am I standing on this frigid porch
in my pajamas, peering into the mist
which rises in little spirals from the pond?
Where they call from the blue
has nearly thinned to no-colour-
clear. Where
they call form hominids haven't yet
happened. Garroo:
who can bear those star-river distances?
I'm so lonesome I could die
happy.

Portrait of Hans Jaegger II (1943)

This lithograph shows the bohemian—decades dead before Munch made his picture—with beneficent face from beneath a hat. It is especially Jaeger's mouth that carries kindness. It smiles and even Jaeger's beard wins friendship. We know Jaeger was hardly always kind, Munch on occasion hated him. But Jaeger conceived in the artist what was most central to him, what belonged at last to him. And we see our helpers in just this light, as when sun mollifies fallen pine needles and illuminates, as with final looks of mercy, the flanks of birches. There is no judgement on what *bohemian* may imply, pain Jaeger may have dealt out. Softest apocalypse, gratitude is lighting after all. If God existed, would God with gratitude look on us? Worshippers are told: be grateful to God; but perhaps God it is who is grateful. Perhaps God comes to God because a true God sees with such eyes of gratitude. The Romans might say Munch himself was near divine by the time he did this lithograph, for Romans called the dead by the name of divine and blessed, *divus*. Perpetual Jaeger, he is the divinity who regards old Munch with young benevolence.

Roadside Vegetable Stand, Outskirts of Kitchener

It sits: it is part of the weather.
It looks forgotten, and reforgotten.
I have never seen it bear fruit;
I have never seen a child man the stand,
selling cabbages or pumpkins.
I have seen it alone,
contemplative,
under a sun that bleaches it blander,
that usurps the green, tattered canopy,
out in the rain that beats it into loneliness.

A farmer might have left it for a moment,
planning to return, and he fell in love with foreclosure,
and the field offers us this stand:
a serious house on serious earth it is,
and it might have been an emporium
of the farmer's first kiss,
or his first inclination to damn it all.

It has stood for years, and has stood for
one good reason: our drive-by appetites withstand care,
and the roadside is one idea of order,
is fifteen years ago when the produce was heavy
and the farmer did not abandon his worry
on the lee side of Hwy. 9, instead
he sold it to us.

Super's Report

Weeds discovered huddled at the tower's base, in cracks,
Were gassed. At last inspection, none had sprung back.

Feisty but mortal, a gangsta tag was wiped
From the north wall, leaving the merest smear, like that on an elder's bib.

Some vague flaw vexing an exec's view—an amendable warp
In her office window's plexiglass—was rendered void by torch.

All seems well and the marble's polish gleams unscuffed and chipper.
The dining room revolves, revealing dreamy views of gloaming vista.

So I sign off, yours truly, humble super bowing out,
Handing my torch to the night shift guy with his paunch and laden belt.

The chimes of his keys will chatter in halls until the dawn's cheeks blush.
His nametag will be accurate, his hounds on their leash robust.

Let's turn in, those hordes of us who need not know the night;
Snore ensconced among the folds of Incident Logs unfilled.

Dozing let's patrol the fabled room immune to grime, or sweep
With brittle straw the pristine floor that greets the newborn feet.

Pupils shifting under lids, wait, wait for the report:
The gun that starts the race, or kills the lights.

Café in Bodrum

Season's end. The seaside patio
is scuttled with upturned chairs.
Piped-in pop tunes crackle out
mid-song as the call to prayer begins.
Flags sigh in the silence, lift
and drop—a crescent, a star,
a crescent, a star—as a cat yawns,
scratches its ear, squinting
from the cool earth in a terracotta pot.
Ribbons of the laid-back cooling tide
stroke the harbour wall, levelled out
and listless as tourists' thoughts,
which are nowhere and everywhere.
Down market lanes, scooters
ferry hot pide and hoick dry coughs
of grey exhaust over the interlocking stones.
No future can be delivered
so effortlessly, despite party slogans
clipped to each lamppost and awning
for the last stretch of the coming election,
though History's narrowed eye
might pause to blink
over a cloud of froth on a cappuccino
or these yacht-masts jabbing the azure.
Mausolus is too far to care, his
pestled tomb once a Seventh Wonder.
Now a few fluted column drums
and troughs for drainage
preserve the age, but only
the mind can still descend
these outlines of stairways to pass
through imagined thresholds

into some deserted notion of repose.
We keep our backs to it, as if
for leverage, and meet
the heat of the sun on our faces.

Coal and Roses: A Triple Glosa

1

Everything is plundered, betrayed, sold,
Death's great black wing scrapes the air,
Misery gnaws to the bone.
Why then do we not despair?

Everything is Plundered . . . Anna Akhmatova Tr. Stanley Kunitz and Max
Hayward

I read the papers with my morning coffee.
Only the horoscope columns offer hope.
We sell our country piecemeal to our neighbour.
Our natural resources are going, going, gone—
our oil, our gas, our water, clear-cut forests.
We dynamite glaciers in our greed for gold.
Polar bears seeking ice floes, swim and drown.
The pillars of our society are felons
and to those of us who knew a more innocent world,
everything is plundered, betrayed, sold.

How many children, this week, shot their mothers?
How many mothers drowned their two-year-olds?
Car bombs account for many, cluster bombs.
Madmen shoot up classrooms, shoot themselves.
This week's body bags again outnumber
the body bags of last week Who can bear
those plastic-wrapped, young, beautiful, rigid corpses
shipped to their grieving girl friends, pregnant wives?
My armband weeps, I weep, and everywhere
death's great black wing scrapes the air.

Street people line the sidewalks, homeless people,
hands out, begging—the unemployable
with all hope gone. Go on, take a dare—
stare in those vacant eyes that gaze on nothing
but heartache, hunger, unimaginable despair.
His Honor, the Mayor of our bustling town,
complains they are ruining the tourist business,
their visibility—a mortal sin
against the holy dollar. O God, where have you gone?
Misery gnaws to the bone.

Prices go up and up. The rich are richer,
la dolce vita in every household, gourmet fare
ordered from gourmet take-outs. The new kitchen,
now an appliance showcase, gadgets galore,
high tech, electric. Hydro cuts a bagel!
Alarm systems only increase our fear.
What are we locking out? our kids on crack?
thieves with fire arms? the all-enveloping dark?
Terrorism brandishes weapons everywhere.
Why then do we not despair?

2

By day, from the surrounding woods,
cherries blow the summer into town;
at night the deep transparent skies
glitter with new galaxies.

Everything is Plundered . . . Anna Akhmatova Tr. Stanley Kunitz and Max
Hayward

Perhaps the crocus, with its furry presence
pushing toward the sunlight through the snow

offers us hope that the whole world is waking
and making music. Tulips, daffodils
narcissus, jonquils, hyacinths, all the bulbs
that paint the air and cram the flowerbeds
sweet talk us into festival and folly.
By night, a fragrant vegetable scent
hovers above the new thin summer bedspreads.
By day, from the surrounding woods

bird calls sound. Nest building is beginning.
Fledglings will hatch and fly. The seasons turn
in ordered, immemorial procession.
Despite excessive rains, power cuts and winds
of hurricane proportions—this is spring:
the longed-for after-winter everyone
was dreaming during those dark months of waiting—
an alternate reality, a bright wing.
And suddenly the grass is overgrown,
cherries blow the summer into town

and kids wear shorts and singlets, and pale girls
search out last years' sandals, part their hair
the other side perhaps, pubescent boys
buy after-shave and condoms. Everywhere
there is a shine, rain glistens, threads of sun
are weaving multicoloured tapestries
spiders spin webs, even the dung beetle
dreams his own small wonderful dream of heaven.
By day the universe is like a kiss,
at night the deep transparent skies

carry us upwards, outwards, into space.
Lie on your back on cooling grass and stare.
Like Zeus, the Perseids shower us with their gold,

and "look!" we cry and "look!" They come so close
they almost touch us and their pale, cold fire
links us with heaven and the Pleiades.
Flesh is forgotten; gone the hoof and horn,
the claw, the canine teeth, the bitter blood
as overhead the deepening darknesses
glitter with new galaxies.

3

And the miraculous comes so close
to the ruined, dirty house—
something not known to anyone at all
but wild in our breast for centuries.

Everything is Plundered . . . Anna Akhmatova Tr. Stanley Kunitz and Max
Hayward

There is a place, not here, not there. No dream
nor opiate can conjure it—it is
not heaven, though heavenly—it is its own
element—not sea, not earth, not air,
nothing approximate, nor half way matched,
where other laws prevail. It honours those
who enter it like water, without wish
vainglorious or trivial—a gift
from realms of outer unimagined space.
And the miraculous comes so close

it alters us. It is as if a beam
embraced us and transformed our molecules
and merged us with some cosmological
and fractal universe we never dreamed,

more vast than any thought we had of love
divine or secular, a synthesis
of right and wrong, of midday, midnight, dawn,
of poverty and wealth, sackcloth and silk.
A gift of coal and roses
to the ruined, dirty houses

and to their opposites—the shining palaces
floating above in towers of cumulus—
that take on size the way a child's balloon
can fill with breath, or perfume scent a room.
This beam--not tenuous nor crystalline,
minus proportions, neither large nor small—
is all encompassing, a kind of womb
a "heaven-haven" and improbable,
some entity beyond recall.
Something not known to anyone at all.

And yet it is our heartbeat, intimate
and human. Here, my wrist—its pulse
is yours for the taking, yet it is not yours.
We share a heartbeat, share lub-dub, lub-dub.
All races, genders, share that little drum
and share its Drummer and its mysteries.
This quiet clock, unnoticed day by day,
our ghost attendant, is invisible,
untouchable, perhaps sublunary,
but wild in our breast for centuries.

Two Cowboys

He yanked the child along,
six years old? dressed like him—
ebony snakeskin boots
scuttling through blaring cabs;
black bolos fluttering;
hats bobbing, black rolled brims.

Were they running late for a wake?
The father scowled. His nose
was gnarled, a boxer's;
blond ponytail fraying, slicked.
The boy tried to keep pace—
skittered along on scuffed toes,

lurched off a curb. The man
swore, quickening his stride.
Oh not to be left behind
when all you clutch is one hand!
Was the boy saddlebag freight
flung on for aching rides?

At the light, he glanced towards me.
Brown colt-eyes, wary, full.
Let him be dashing from shifts
at the fair's Wild West tent.
Let me not find him years on
tossed, by broken bulls.

Before

In the woods an hour ago,
I found bearberry—
do you remember what they call
kinnickinnick? Of course
you remember. The small
sticky leaves clinging to my face,
that summer, years ago, when I came up
from beneath you.
      This was before
any of the catastrophes.
We were far from innocent,
but we were, yes,
     unknowing.
Your body shines, glistens, in memory,
as you lie back on the bed of moss
and I approach, bare feet wet from the lake,
and kneel. I look up once
at the backdrop of white spruce
and resinous wind, and look down,
and cover you.

A line returns now, a fragment
from what I tried to write
afterwards: *you*
can only get there by water.
I still hope to use it, to play
with how it breaks:
     you can only
get there by water. I'll punctuate this
with the real and the imagined.
I can clearly see how the leaves
on my cheeks became green-flecked

motes in your eyes
                    and then in mine.
And you alone know the texture and shade
of moss beneath my hips, the foliage
over my shoulder, and how
the wind insinuates between us
when we draw apart, as we wade
into the shallows, warm and cool
and warm.
                    We pull on our clothes
while we're still wet, stepping into the boat
and pushing off. How buoyant we were
for days after.
                    I'm going to say it now,
are you listening? You can only get there
by water.

Big News Café

Corner of Granville Street and Broadway with Kaplan Business college brick parapet, white neon letters scrawled on blue revolving sign. Sand brick with stone moulding and blue accents. Row of churchy pointed windows and brick piers modernism condemned. Not structural, so no right to appear with their peaked gables. Two enormous churchy-pointed arches over main entrance. Stone crests on either side, narrow twisted columns with scroll-top capitals dreaming of quadrangles at Oxford. QAT, DAT, SAT, PCAT, GMAT window signs. To Idle Ant in Big News Café. Horoscope: *by all means help someone in dire need. Rush in like the knight in shining armour you've always wanted to be. But don't promise to bail them out unless you want them ringing you up morning, noon and night.*

Shining-armour Don Quixote Ant stares through café glass for big news—some Polaris or Cassiopeia for dead reckoning—haut shops on Lord Large-village street, Blenz Coffee under Business College. All merged in a big dream. Northeast corner, Royal Bank. Southwest corner, Chapters Books. Big boxes selling little cartons of fancy. *RSPs make all your retirement dreams come true.* The bank's yellow letters, black marble facing on concrete slabs and rows of aluminum windows.

City's a lot of going into—rooms—wombs. Non-city's one big space. In Shining-armour Ant-mind.

The Ocean Voyager

In memory of John and Ralph Wilson

Comes the wayward waters of the coast
Bearing me on its unbroken back, chartless,
Without compass or sextant, no ghost
Or unseen hand guiding me by cutlass

Or caress: I enter Hecate the only captain
This vessel will ever know—to hell
With illness-stitched wool, English pain
Balled in musket shot, delicate otter shells

Piled like money in the hold, I sold
The treacherous lot to the sea, the boatmen
Tagged and taken by whitecaps, lassoed
To the beach, wrecked and erected as totems

By panther-eyed armies of salal and skin,
Omens for the coming centuries painted
The ever green of cedar and greed. No sin
Shone from a lantern's idiot eye; no tainted

Light spewed from the moon, splattering
In the Pacific mist like insects. Darkness kissed
The phosphorescent salmon chattering
At my hull and scrubbed the stains of piss

And wine and filthy commerce from my deck.
Emptier than a child's mind, I made
The scrambled brains of Desolation on-spec
My thirteenth day where the tidal braid

Of the strait cradled and rocked me to sleep
Like your whisky. A pale bag of deer
Bobbed at my ribs, uncorked from the deep
Well of the lived. I danced troughs like fear

On nervous highways, two-stepped crests
Like early love, and since then I have flown
Lightning wracked seas in the fissured west,
Known what men thought they've known.

The low sun slouching steadily toward Japan
Dragging white contrails across the screen
Of the atmosphere, the sea's eyelids frozen
Shut by shards of stars, the maddened screed

Of waves like buffalo stampeding to oblivion
Upon the shore. I have dreamed the curdled
Hand of ice in harbour, for the nattering wind
A muzzle, crows hauling dawn across the world.

To be sure, I've hunted Haida Gwaii like
A hound, nosed its Monkey Beach with my keel
Then turned on the wheel of the ocean, flocks
Of Glaucous in the endless seas above reeling

With me, southward through the kelp-nets
And fermenting weeds, the forever drizzle
Like chains hanging from heaven's basement.
Orca offal in the tidal flats, the mud's missal

Of decay and puzzle, a rotting hull of ribcage.
I note these things along the way, a hoard
To lord over and over, arrange a rearrange
Upon the galley-bench of mind searching for

Order. Glinting teeth of glaciers cut seawards
Over thousands of years but I will not rudder
Or tack here and no creature nor any words
Alive today will be so when these beasts shudder

And make their move to water. I would
Show children those oolichan like candles
Burning beneath the surface, the driftwood
Castles yet to be imagined on the beach, mantles

Of foam and salt the drowned will shoulder
Like boas from a rubber tree. On my gunnels
Dance shore birds the weight of a lust-whisper
In the ear. Comes running through runnels

Of air, the landfall gossip: floating islands
Like glass fishing globes snatched from the map
For souvenirs. Water-drunk, sea-canned
By briny slosh, my staves won't rot or snap

And release me finally to the silent squelch
Of the depths, fathoms beneath in the birdless
Pitch where I would remain like a ship's wench
On her knees, gladly, to be relieved of the aegis

Of my own fate, saved from the sobbing breast
I have suckled to long now with its shadow
Flowers and jelly-wasps; no old galleon guest
On this coast nor armoured monitor would know

To dredge the surface for my prow; riddled
With lichens of pale sun, barnacle-tumours,
Azure phlegm, I drift of my own unbridled
Arrogance never coming up against the rumoured

Wall of the sky reddened by the savage blood
Of pilgrims beating their heads out of this
Labyrinth-mine. I've weathered tsunami and flood,
Maelstroms of fifty twisted leagues, behemoths

Of wind hammering nights sidereal architecture
Its scuddering floes of clouds skewered on
Mountain parapets, the firmaments fractured
And opened to swallow sailors and all gone

Wanderers save me. Is it such elemental
Rapture that you exist, exiled with the golden
Plover, the lapwing, caught in the career and pull
Of there to there and never anywhere you happen

To be, simply, at the moment? I fear the acrid
Torpor of this love. I desire a black pond
Of frogspawn, a sad child burdened by limpid
Eyes folding an origami boat to chart reed fronds,

Or a mayfly cocooned in paper and set free
By fingers from the prison-ship of its first form.
Such forlorn languor as I call home, I do not see
History's electric Diogenes pass over me in alarm.

To Darwin in Chile, 1835

You will learn to look on every city as Venice,
stone lofted for a while as sun-draped statue before
the tide grinds it to sand. Viewed through the telescopic

glass of geology, mountains collapse to seabeds,
reptiles leave to return as hummingbirds, scallop shells
arise in their brittle white gowns to haunt hilltops banked

over the bones of whales. Yet now, alift with earthquake,
floating on dry land is new to you: "Earth, the emblem
of all that is solid, moves beneath our feet, a crust

over a fluid." You are a skater on wafer-
thin ice, or a ship skidding over a cross-ripple.
The Cathedral's portal, tilted seawards, is a prow

of arched oak scudding over bobbing rubble. So much
for founding a church on a rock, you think, when keystones
founder, crack, split, fragment. Even the hand-picked Peter

broke in a single night, cock-crow finding him marooned
in a wreckage of denial. Yet if you could call
together all the coloured crystals of the east wall's

stained glass window—most benign form of rock, stone's thinnest
shadow, now shattered to stardust—you would see your life's
and this moment's discoveries lightly prefigured

in the image of another storm-tossed man whose feet
tested earth's rocky sediment and found it seafoam,
walking on water as you do now, as we all do.

Echoes in November

Correspondences are everywhere,
things that shadow things,
that breathe or borrow
essence not their own;
and so the yellow leaves
that, singly, streak
in silence past a black
uncurtained pane
(catching the lamplight from within
as they dart down)
have the elusiveness
of shooting stars,
and so it sometimes happens
that you pause
in kitchen ministrations,
knife in hand
above the chopping board,
savouring, raw, a stub
of vegetable not destined
for the pot,
and faintly tasting
at the back of the palate
the ghost of a rose
in the core of the carrot.

Breathing Exercise: A How-To Poem

For Gil Fronsdal
and in memory of Mark O'Brien (1949-1999)

The distance between the brightness
at the top of the spine
and the darkness below it

is not far
but when you shrink your mind
it is enormous

the whole length
of human history
can be fit inside it

One way to reduce it a little
is with practice and preparation

(the latter takes minutes each morning
the former has taken me years)

is to gather the sensations in our belly
into our in-breath

(do this slowly and with enjoyment
that darkness deep inside us
should be like the jungle in Thailand

where we may acknowledge the presence
of unseen pythons and kraits

but our actual sensations
as we search the deep canopy
for crimson sunbirds

are of lazy butterflies
and flowering lianas)

and then by a skilled relaxing
of both muscle and nerve
guide our breathing

slowly up the back of our spine
so that it breaks over the top
like a wave breaking over a quiet beach

to drench the scattered thoughts
spread out to no purpose
and then draw them slowly back down

in the descent of the out-breath
to the dark easy rhythm

of the untiring diaphragm
where the in-breath began

Relax the spaces in between
each vertebra
let each space slightly expand

until in each out-breath
you can exhale *metta*   *compassion*

commingling the cool light
and warm darkness

to those whom you usually consider
enemies and friends

Before Leaving Hué

On the Thien Mu Pagoda sacred grounds
a young monk, bald with the slimmest of arms
sits in the shade of frangipani trees
where songbirds harmonize the afternoon's
intense humidity and addresses me,
his voice a gong's lingering vibration
his English soft yet penetrating,
"You must visit Thúy before you leave Hué."

I'm walking to the relic on display
a rusting blue car driven by the monk
who set himself on fire in '63.
Tomorrow's my last day in this city
devoted to its poets, their verses
woven into conical hats that shield
the scars of mines and agent orange.
I follow the bleached path back to the piers
to board a blue and yellow dragon boat
as sunset streaks the Perfume River sky.
The boatman steers through swirling currents
then cuts the motor to save gas. We float
with purpose, direction, but in no rush.
He docks, I rise to disembark and pay,
ten thousand sorrows map the boatman's eyes.
"Please visit Thúy," he says, "before leaving Hué."

I savour my last night's meal in Hué
seated on wicker by riverside lights,
not a pinch of the vague in the chilies,
turmeric, fish sauce and roasted cashews
balanced by sweet, potent *café glacé*.
An ancient woman, frail yet dignified

in her white silk *ao dai*, slips me Thúy's card
with a whisper, *"Il faut la visiter."*

Under the hammer of Hué's morning sun
my *xích lô* driver pedals the labyrinth
of streets and alleys, past shadowy shops
where raw silks hang inert, dazed by the heat.
We skid on the puddles and pebbled ruts
and I gesture, "Let me walk the rest" but
he cycles on, eyes glazed, body bent by
psychic will that I visit Thúy today.

I find her inside a concrete shack
seated in a dome of lemony sun
shafting sideways through one paneless window.
In a slow motioned circle around her
women prepare palm leaves, cut threads and twill,
smooth back loosened strands of her fine black hair.
I'm seated on a stool in the corner
as if awaited by Thúy on my last day
as if she understands that all of Hué
has sent me here to witness the making
of a poem, a sacred act in this place
where suffering spans centuries of stanzas.
She bows over the work between her feet,
images and words cut from black paper.
Among layers of translucent palm leaves
Thúy weaves her cosmos, weightless yet concrete.

Hours of sweat before she's satisfied
and the poem is offered into sunlight
revealing silhouettes of lovers lost,
songbirds and a riverside pagoda,
six lines of verse in Vietnamese.

She points with her one arm, it is handless,
at the embedded name I won't forget,
Thúy, the poet I met before leaving Hué.

Tractor

More than a storey high and twice that long,
it looks igneous, the Buhler Versatile 2360,
possessed of the ecology of some hellacious
minor island on which options
are now standard. Cresting the sections
in a corona part dirt, part heat, it appears
risen full-blown from our deeper needs,
aspiring its turbo-cooled air, articulated
and fully compatible. What used to take a week
it does in a day on approximately
a half-mile to the gallon. It cost one hundred
fifty grand. We hope to own it outright by 2017.
Few things wrought by human hands
are more sublime than the Buhler Versatile 2360.

Across the road, a crew erects the floodlit
derricks of a Texan outfit whose presumptions
are consistently vindicated.
The ancient sea bed will be fractured to 1000 feet
by pressuring through a pipe literal tons
of a fluid—the constituents of which
are best left out of this —
to tap the sweet gas where it lies like the side
our bread is buttered on. The earth shakes
terribly then, dear Houston, dear parent
corporation, with its re-broken dead and freshly
killed, the air concussive, cardiac, irregular.
It silences the arguments of every living thing
and our minds in that time are not entirely elsewhere.

But I was speaking of the Buhler Versatile 2360
Phase D! And how well recognized it is among the classics: Wagner,
Steiger, International Harvester, John Deere, Case,
Minneapolis-Moline, Oliver, White, Allis-Chalmers,
Massey-Ferguson, Ford, Rite, Rome.
One could say it manifests fate, cast
like a pearl around the grit of centuries. That,
in a sense, it's always been with us,
the diesel smell of a foregone conclusion.
In times of doubt, we cast our eyes
upon the Buhler Versatile 2360
and are comforted. And when it breaks down, or thinks
itself in gear and won't, for our own good, start,
it takes a guy out from the city at 60 bucks an hour
plus travel and parts, to fix it.

Pugnax Gives Notice

He's done with it, the tridents and tigers,
the manager's greed, the sumptuous beds
of noble women who please their own moods.
He's done with dogging it for the crowds,
the stabbing, the slashing, the strangling,
the poor pay, the chintzy palm branch prizes.
Make no mistake. Pugnax is a real fierceosaurus.
Winner of 26 matches, a forum favourite.
Yet his yob genes have, it seems, gone quiet.
Fatigue has called his soul back to his body.
Circles under his eyes; he sleeps badly.
Late-night cigs lit from the dog-end of the last,
cutwork of the clock nibbling him small.
In the barracks around him his friends snore,
lucky returnees of the last hard hacking,
dead to the world, free of a weapon in the fist.
Priscus face-down in the crook of his arm.
Triumphus flung open, caught on a bad turn.
Verus collapsed, whacked, against the cot.
Flamma, doomed by down-thumbing shadows,
lies in a stain of his final shape and size.
Pugnax loves them all, chasers and net-fighters,
fish-men and javelin-throwers, carefree
despite punishing practices, screaming orders,
despite limbs trained to turn lethal for mobs
unable to bear the thought of two men
clinging to life, but here it's only the thock
of wooden sword against wooden sword,
the racket as they fall on each other's shields
in joy. Pugnax's heart breaks for them.

Understand, he has inflicted pain and felt pain,
but now wants to go native, move into a flat,
experiment with fashionable clothes,
dawdle at the baths, tame his nights with tea,
be spellbound by the smell of soap, find a wife.
Our boy dreams of joining the crowd,
shouting himself hoarse as some bonehead
gets knocked down and the blade pushed
though his chest, stapling him to the ground.
At intermission, he'll watch as the blood
is raked over with sand, thinking chore thoughts:
yard work, paint jobs, weekend projects.

Beating the Bounds

When I was six years old, my parents,
along with other adults who'd never spoken
to me, came laughing and acting silly,
picking me up, giggling, "Now we'll show
you a house you didn't now about."
"A big house."
"A secret house you knew about all the time."
So I was frightened, seeing how serious
it was that they were so strange,
although I was probably smiling,
and they carried me and other children my age
to the river and said, "Here is the marble
floor," and put my bare legs in the fast
place between stones and it was colder
than I remembered it and the tugging of dark
cold water became my legs, the Fox Island
River became my legs—afterwards when I
was falling asleep or sometimes just walking
along, the bottom of me would be moving away
like that—and they carried me tickling me
singing ridiculous songs among rough
brown stones up a valley past caribou
where it was cold and held me up on top
of their palms so I faced the sky and someone
with fat fingers that smelled of sheep held
my eyes open so that cold air and the white
sky burned and were too bright and my eyes
brimmed like two cuts and I felt those cuts
go right into my name and they said
"This is the roof up here, you can't go
higher than this," and that wind and sky
were my eyes then, they were in my name,

and the people pushed me through a patch
of alders and a patch of spruce the wind
had bent, saying, "Here's a young cub
we'll take home and raise," and "Push him in front
so we won't get scratched," and my skin
was crisscrossed with cuts, so I felt
those branches, smelled the alder musk,
the sharp edge of spruce like a coast,
a burning fringe, a noise around me holding
me in and they said, "This is the west
wall of the house you live in, remember
it," and the day went on like that, they
pushed me against a cliff to the north
so I felt its jaggedness in my spine,
they sad me in black soupy peat and said,
"Here is your bed, it is night time," they
took me down to the sea and made me
drink it and told me that was the south
and the kitchen, "the garden" someone
laughed and gave me a capelin to eat, rubbed
scales on my face, the backs of my hands
and "Over here," they said, meaning
over the hills across the gulf, "that is not
your house and the people who live there
are strangers to you, not enemies if
you deal with them properly." "They
speak a language of farts," someone said,
"they gobble like turkeys when they fuck,"
and although my body was made of all
it had touched that day and my ears were full
of my parents' voices and the voices
of their friends, in my heart I was still
frightened and felt like a stranger among them.

New Canaan

A hummer, a whistler, a man
bent on keeping the blues at bay,
at the slightest peep from sorrow
he turns tail and runs away
lacking perhaps some enzyme
to properly process grief
as any undercurrent of discord
throws him into such a funk
his passport is at the ready
as are contingency plans
to leave at the drop of a hat
should the heat in the kitchen rise
and he find himself again,
unravelled or unsteady
but shouldn't he know by now
that as fast as he might go
trouble hitches a ride in his pocket
and to prove it he might remember this:

The universe practically hummed
when they met and she said
we are standing smack on the fault
and my name is, guess what, Andrea
and our meeting 's been foretold
to this very hour and day
three weeks ago by her astrologist
who dropped acid and his MBA
to train in an ashram in India
and was, you know, into stars,
for Venus was ascending
and Saturn transiting through
my second house, the house of wealth,

but she took wealth to mean just love
and that a van would be leaving soon
so, here, take a long puff on this,
and tomorrow, under a new moon,
they could both be in New Canaan
and would he like to come along
and he said he would and he did.

Everyone a vegetarian,
coffee strictly *verboten*,
the commune was not for him
and though he liked the sex
he cared little for the hours,
waking up with the roosters
to meditate on empty stomachs
while bad breath and night odours
were not exactly conducive
to the aimed-for transcendence
insisting, as they did, the body
holds the spirit in a hammer lock
and is not about to let go
and his the worst of all
for when they sat down to their gruel
his loquacious stomach growled
in such long, drawn out sentences
he took to calling it Cicero
and when sent into town for feed
he was caught at the local Wendy's
and the camel's back was broken
for Brother Bill hauled him in,
asked him to leave and he did
with no time to say bye to Andrea.

Unjust, unjust he sensed right away
this caricature of Andrea
drawn some forty years to the day
they first met at the fault line
for he had soon recognized
she had qualities he sorely lacked
such as, for instance, a backbone,
he who drifted like a jelly fish
and though she never accused
he could sense the disappointment
when she tracked him down
five or six years after Canaan
to find him stalled at a dead end
running errands across the border
for the sleazebag, Dr. Ramon,
proof positive that you can run
and yet stand still, while she
after leaving the commune,
finished a nursing degree
and made ready to ship out
to work in a village in Africa
from where she would never return.

The Highway That Became a Footpath

(after the other side won the civic election)

And I saw a new heaven and a new earth,
for the first heaven and the first earth had passed away,
and I saw the holy city, coming down out of heaven . . .
and the holy raving protester who climbed into a tree
to resist the building of the last highway
was still in among the leaves,
but the tree had grown much taller,
and the protester had been living up there for such a long time,
not alone, that several generations of protesters now populated the canopy,
freely trafficking the branches of their swaying neighbourhoods,
as the six-lane highway
wound between the trunks below
as wide only as a footpath,
a red-dirt earthway, busy with pedestrians.
And the highway-that-became-a-footpath
led past the longhouse raised
during the same resistance, down in the valley,
for it still existed (both longhouse *and* valley existed still)
and other longhouses,
which were standing at that location several centuries earlier,
had re-materialized, their hearth-fires
burning still; an entire village, thriving
beside the hallowed creek that ran through the east end of the city.
And I saw the trees that formed the longhouse walls
take root, and continue to grow,
forty thousand times forty thousand,
their canopy providing all the roof
that the people needed.
And from a privileged perch at the top of the escarpment,

watching as the new city came down out of heaven,
it was clear that the leaves of those trees
were for the healing of the community.

The Celebration

Was it a poorly attended event, a celebration
no one felt like celebrating? Was there no
live music? Was there
a table with small empanadas
and cubes of cheese, another with bottles of wine?
Had the winter day subsided into early
evening before the rush hour, white wine
larking in your bloodstream as you
walk to the parking lot? The prawns
had been large and plump, sweet.
Could we have eaten a dozen?
And besides, it turned out
that so-and-so had been born in
a small Eurasian town. Which of the following
instruments were generally played by popular persons?
(a) accordion
(b) banjo
(c) piano

Was crockery flung at the mantel? Did they dance
with throats proud and uplifted?

Were they enjoined to celebrate some government policy or other?
Daycare day, eat broccoli day, safety day! Apology day! Not worrying
about anything day! Old guys driving vintage cars in the slow lane!
    Young guys at
the Keg on a big night out! Catholics playing six cards each at
the bingo hall! Insomniacs fretting with camomile in the kitchen!
Old men weeping in the parks! Boys sobbing in armies! Moloch, Moloch,
celebration in Moloch! Travellers picking at room service chicken pot pies!
Underpaid clerks helpful at the insurance office! Hermaphodite trout!
Box stores with irritable cashiers! Pepsi salesmen analyzing flow charts!

Grandmas eyeing the sherry! Orangutans grieving in zoos! Secretaries!
Undertakers!
Robots on the telephone! Oral hygienists! English professors
    defeated by poesie!
Celebrate! Celebrate!

The moon keeps us company all the way home, her dark smile and
    brocade blouse.
We saw her coming over the hills and ducked into
the collar of our coat. We know perfectly well we could use a little
of her scorn, her glamour.

Nightingale

Maximilian is mad for the end of the world. In his spare time, he writes fake obituaries for people he has loved. Wednesday, it's his Grade 3 teacher, Mrs Weemer, whose overturned-bowl-shaped eyes made his throat choke up. Max takes care with his words, works in an allusion to Florence Nightingale because she was the day's Final Jeopardy! question. The winning contestant wrote *what* instead of *who*, and Max hissed at the TV. Stupid paralegals—no survival skills. When nuclear winter arrives on their doorstep, they'll be fuelling up the snowblower. Fire, ice, it's all the same to him, as long as he gets a grenade launcher. He finishes up the obit just before his shift: "Life bullies only those with tender souls." Coming home from work early in the a.m., he pauses beside a guy asleep on the subway grate. Max is still wearing his Kinko's name tag, so he pretends to drop change in the coffee cup, kicks it over instead. Crosses the street quick as he can, coins still inside his head. Then he remembers Mrs Weemer, scrubbing at his little scraped palms, trying to keep up with his sobs, and holds on tight. The spilt milk of her eyes. She's a dead woman, he thinks.

O Brother

Leave off your blasted syntax, biker,
your straight-pipe exhaust of a mouthpiece,
your frayed flag flapping-hard manifesto.

I make a hex on you with my flannel pants,
with my side-parted hair, my in bed by eleven,
my yen for ideals, for love, for my children.

It will call you at dusk to my brightly lit window,
make you stare in until drapes are drawn,
make you harbour these thoughts:

Profound the bikes abandoned on lawns
and the shrieks of children shaking free
their last few kilowatts of energy.

Together lets blast off for the unknown,
out of the been-there-done-that zone,
and over the bluffs of who's kidding whom.

TOM WAYMAN

Teaching English

What does English not know
that it needs to hear from me? So many instructors
have drawn its attention to the absurd spelling,
how chopping a tree down
is not the opposite of chopping a tree up.
The language has endured enough talk
about the "they're"/"their"/"there" wackiness
and users' continual bafflement
over the purpose of the apostrophe.

Can I convey anything
to help English function better
where it earns a paycheque
or during intimate encounters?
I regard it, scratch my head.
It stares back at me while it sits,
headphones on, earbuds pumping music
directly into the auditory nerve,
vocabulary shrinking along with
cognitive ability—consequence of too much television
before age three, perhaps, or excessive cellphone use
—eyes blank
as a missing comma.

July Baby

Why can't we be more like the dandelion,
hollow-stemmed, milky-sapped?
Wouldn't sex be sexier if sex were asexual?
Just because we possess
stamens and pistils
doesn't mean
we have to use them.
Let's fertilize ourselves.
What's the evolutionary advantage
of going ga-ga and wobbly in the knees?
Don't you get tired of the complex human complexities?
Why can't we travel
all night on an all-night train
and wake up as something else, a taproot, say.
Let's be savvy and adaptive and flaunt
our tiny florets. Wouldn't you rather
by-pass the awkward introductions
and clone yourself?
Don't think *invasive weed*,
think *fairy clock, rosette of deeply-lobed leaves.*
It might be fun to pop up
unwelcome and anywhere,
the front lawn of City Hall.
Why can't we be more like the humble
dandelion in a field of humble dandelions?
Who says you can't throw off
your body and float like a filament
in the summer wind? Let's get drunk
as puffballs in a roadside ditch.
Let's make summer babies without reproductive organs
or classes in synchronized breathing.
Three days old, this one lies on a blanket

beneath the maple tree. Oh prince
of the meadow, oh bright
yellow flower-head!

Chinese Chimes: Nine Detours of the Yellow River

you are unaware of your obscure sources
but you are explicitly sure of the vast sea
    as your final destination

    you always frown with your brownish wrinkles
    but you prefer a nonprofessional smile on your face
        your only luggage of life

        all your teeth have been lost or pulled out
        but you keep licking the muddy banks with your heart
            despite your dreams forged

    your song is no more than a foam of silence
but you struggle hard to remain afloat on the sea of noise
    beyond the borderline of heaven

your love for the loess plateau often overturns and overflows
    but you have never flooded the valley of the dragon's mind
                since confucius's times

    your course ahead is crowded with holes and crevices
        but you will deliver your promises to every unevenness
        instead of promising the deliveries only

        you occupy an enormously tiny place of the world
but you feed all the hopes and wishes of those
            with thirsty mouths stranded ashore

    you flow down from the sky created by yourself
but you hope to avoid falling on the broken floor
        of your own church

you may be tortured or burned to steam
but you will eventually find your impossible way
            to the sea of blue sky

Practising Bach

for performance with Bach's E Major Partita for Solo Violin, BWV1006

Prelude

There is, said Pythagoras, a sound
the planet makes: a kind of music
just outside our hearing, the proportion
and the resonance of things—not
the clang of theory or the wuthering
of human speech, not even
the bright song of sex or hunger, but
the unrung ringing that
supports them all.

The wife, no warning, dead
when you come home. Ducats
in the fishheads that you salvage
from the rubbish heap. Is the cosmos
laughing at us? No. It's saying

improvise. Everywhere you look
there's beauty, and it's rimed
with death. If you find injustice
you'll find humans, and this means
that if you listen, you'll find love.
The substance of the world is light,
is water: here, clear
even when it's dying; even when the dying
seems unbearable, it runs.

Loure

Why is Bach's music more like speech than any other? Because of
its wisdom, I think. Which means its tempering of lyric passion by
domesticity, its grounding of the flash of lyric insight in domestic
earth, the turf of dailiness.

Let us think of music as a geometry of the emotions. Bach's
practice, then, resembles that of the Egyptians: earth's measure as a
way of charting the bottomlands of the Nile, the floodwaters of the
heart, as a way of charting life. Opera, Greek tragedy, Romantic poetry
tell us that sex and death are what we have to focus on if we want to
understand any of the rest. Bach's music, by contrast, speaks directly
to, and of, life itself—the resonant ground of sex and death.

And it does this not without ornamentation, but without fuss:
the golden ratio in the whelk shell lying on the beach, the leaf whorl
opening to sun, the presence of the divine in the chipped dish drying
in the rack, *that* miracle: good days, bad days, a sick kid, a shaft of
sunlight on the organ bench. *Talk to me, I'm listening.*

Gavotte

E major: June wind
in the buttercups, wild
and bright and tough.
Like luck—a truth
that's on the surface of a thing,
not because it's shallow, but because
it's open: overtoned.
Because it rings.
            Fate, too,
is character. But it's

the shape—the cadence
and the counterpoint. Luck
lives in the moment, and it
looks at you: the clear eye,
gold, when being sings.

Menuet I & II

There's nothing special in it. All you have to do
is hit the right key at the right time. Time:
that stream in which we do, and do not,
live. *Just practise diligently; it will all go well. You have*
five fingers on each hand, just as healthy as my own.
Unison, the octave; the fifth, the fourth, the third.
Of the strings? The viola, if I have a choice.
At the keyboard, don't forget to use your thumb.
God's glory and the recreation of the mind.
What I really need to know:
does the organ have good lungs?
The partita of the world, the dance of being: *everything*
has to be possible.

Bourée

Partita, partie—a whole of many parts. Pythagoras, who is said to
have studied with the Egyptians, is also said to have taught that
enlightenment meant solving the problem of the One and the Many,
of coming to grasp the divine unity of the world through its bits and
pieces, as these come to us in language.

This may also be thought of as the problem of metaphor: that
metaphor's truth, its charge of meaning, depends on assertion of

identity and difference, on erotic coherence and referential strife, on meaning as resonance and meaning revealed through analysis.

Lyric poets are always trying to approach the issue by forcing speech to aspire to the condition of music. Bach comes at it from the other end: he infuses music with a sense of the terrible concreteness, the particularity, of the world. And enlightenment?—Acceptance of, delight in, the mystery of incarnation.

Gigue

There is a sound
that is a whole of many parts,
a sorrowless transparency, like luck,
that opens in the centre of a thing.
An eye, a river, fishheads, death,
gold in your pocket, and a half-wit
son: the substance of the world
is light and blindness and the measure
of our wisdom is our love.
Our diligence: ten fingers and
a healthy set of lungs. Practise
ceaselessly: there is
one art: wind
in the open spaces
grieving, laughing
with us, saying
improvise.

KEVIN CONNOLLY

Last One on the Moon

How could something so rote,
so written, find time to surprise?
Niche of cliché, nemesis of fresh,
yet there it is again, lording it over the
firing dust, silhouettes of trees . . .
Never agreed to be extras, never think of
themselves as frames, never thought a thing
except in this drowsy context, which
morphs into heartfelt syntax, scares that
cynic heart you worship straight.

It's not that you want to stand up there
(you do), it's that it stands you up
in an uncomfortable cold that's always
cold now, on a bike, on a bike path
pressing down, beside a highway suddenly
tragic without its pointless imagined
lunar road signs . . . panting over
spinning wheels, which have never
in your experience struck you as ancient
or orbital, though they are now as
surely as they won't be tomorrow.

Perhaps it speaks to childhood: last one
on the moon's a rotten egg, lost morning,
poor reflection of what happened here
just twenty-one seconds ago, right here beside
you, and bounced back. Wrong? Sure.
Terracentrically incorrect. Any light in that
gray eye could only be the fireball itself.

Except for us, concerned with all those things
thinking wastes: hacks and demons, the
drowned and saved, glad dogs still
digging all these deep hours into night.

Margaret Atwood, "Ice Palace"

In her October 2007 *Toronto Star* review of Margaret Atwood's *The Door*, Barbara Carey wrote, "The chilly, disquieting 'Ice Palace' metaphorically links a luxury hotel with Bluebeard's castle."

Margaret Avison, "Two Whoms or I'm in Two Minds"

In a gently humorous way, Margaret confesses her aversion to generalities, contrasting them with particulars, the "particulates" whom she loves to "dance" among, with "castanets" in her poetry.

Ken Babstock, "Autumn News from The Donkey Sanctuary"

As birthday gift to a friend, we had "adopted" a donkey at a sanctuary near Guelph, Ont. Subsequently, newsletters began arriving in the mail so it was like being sent a Wallace Stevens title minus its accompanying poem. Gift begets gift. It likely opens too close to derivative Stevens, with the named "characters" singing, or chanting, but the intent was to drift near to political allegory while avoiding any single interpretive trap. Agamben's thoughts on *Homo Sacer* float nearby, and by implication critiques of western liberalism's more explicit shortcomings, but also surveillance and safety and domesticity and *verse*. I very nearly dumped this poem before noticing its screeching turn arrives approximately where it would in a sonnet. So, I don't know, levels of illusion embedded in the pastoral. Have finally visited the sanctuary, and am happy to report . . . (?)

Shirley Bear, "Flight"

A lover once bathed in a cold stream for me. It was the most erotic event and the first time anyone ever did this, for me to enjoy. I use to write notes, appointments, birthdays, and sketched in my day minder. It was a convenient sort of "all in one." When I was asked to submit some work to the *West Coast LINE 45*, I re-discovered this poem in one of my many day minders. From my studio in 1,000 Parker Street, Vancouver, BC, I incorporated the present with the past when I submitted the poem and found that it was magical.

Tim Bowling, "1972"

If Frank Sinatra can recollect a very good year, then so can I. In my case, 1972 was a very good year indeed. I was in the midst of a terrific childhood in a beautiful place, Neil Young's pop was on the charts, and late summer's a lovely time for the naturally elegiac. Besides, life always makes us choose: do we want to be grovelling whiners or do we want to be whaleback?

Asa Boxer, "Dante's Ikea"

Any resemblance between Ikea and the Inferno is purely coincidental. For one, Virgil wouldn't be caught dead at Ikea. There are no three-headed dogs at the door. There are far more circles in hell. And you don't need a boat to get around.

Anne Compton, "Even now"

Nature is very clever. It pairs grandchildren and grandparents; there's an acuity of observation in both. While we were playing, my three-year-old grandson asked, "Granny Anne, are you old?" "Even now," prompted by that question, doesn't deny the fact. Nonetheless, it rewrites the pathology of aging, turns its so-called diminishments to something else: the body, as it ages, opens all its sensory pathways. We want, and we take, a greedy drink of the world.

Jan Conn, "Space Is a Temporal Concept"

Mostly I'm a lyrical poet who sometimes slides sideways into a narrative voice. The language cascade and internal rhythm that begins in this capricious poem with the snails resembled white water kayaking: lots of whirlpools, striated rocks, and a few calm stretches, until arriving—exhilarated—at the puppy. Many strands of feelings and images, art and history, collided and jostled for space. There's a fusion of the turbulence and wildness of New York City and two of Paul Klee's enigmatic puppets, Lord Death and the Wide-Eared Clown. Environmental disrepair and Mexican cultures and their ideas of time are themes I revisit often. I didn't invite the goddess Diana to this party but she emerged, at least in profile, possibly to counterbalance my father, who put in a cameo appearance not long after his death. Chance and randomness are major components of my somewhat offbeat voice, perhaps accounting for the roulette wheel and the unexpected pastry chef.

Kevin Connolly, "Last One on the Moon"

As an offbeat, idiomatic, slightly surreal lyricist, I've always been more concerned that my poems be interesting or entertaining as opposed to profound or edifying. Imagine my horror, then, when I discovered at least a half-dozen references to the moon in my 2005 collection, *drift*. How could such a transparently overloaded image slip so easily under my defences? I adopted a self-imposed moratorium on the topic, until one evening, on my way home along the lake on my bicycle, I was hit in the face with an enormous, early-rising moon over Asbridge's Bay: completely extraterrestrial in every sense. The title, "Last One on the Moon," is probably wishful thinking, but I've held out since this poem—so far.

Lorna Crozier, "Mercy"

A few winters ago my husband, Patrick Lane, and I lived in the Wallace Stegner house in Eastend, Saskatchewan. Stegner made the town and its history famous in his marvellous book *Wolfwillow*. The rolling short-grass prairie that rolls from my hometown of Swift Current to Eastend is the landscape that formed my blood and bones over sixty years ago. Almost every night, one of my delights was to listen to the coyotes calling back and forth across the narrow Frenchman's River that forms the town's western border. Unfortunately, not everyone shares my love of these animals. That winter, and no doubt other winters as well, the nearby town of Shaunavon proudly hosted a Coyote Derby, which awarded prizes for the most coyotes shot in a two-week period. Some locals consider the animals "varmits" and think nothing of hunting them down in snowmobiles, roaring behind them until they wear out and flounder. Some sport, isn't it? I wrote "Mercy" after seeing the dead coyotes hanging from a clothes stand in an alley in town. In reality, I was less articulate. I shook my fist at the house and yelled "Assholes!" and sunk into a depression for hours. I wanted to write something that honoured these beautiful singers but didn't turn away from what had happened to them. How beautiful they were, even in death. Some days I feel so ashamed to be human.

Barry Dempster, "Groin"

A visit to the doctor's office, a sense of threatened self, a mild case of shame in having to say the word "groin" to the medical secretary—these hardly seemed like optimum conditions for a poem. But a poem was nonetheless stirring at the very hint of mortality. In fact, the poem was already planning to teach me a thing or two about the lyric impulse having no boundaries, about language and its musical intensities tuning up in the strangest places. "Careful," I whispered to the doctor as he donned his latex gloves, "there's a poem in there and it hurts."

Don Domanski, "Bite Down Little Whisper"

"Bite Down Little Whisper" grew out of a trip I made to the Cape Breton Highlands, the only book I had with me was the *Upanishads*. The passage I quote in the poem was one I kept returning to time and again. It became a kind of touchstone during my stay in the forest and was a real source of comfort for me.

John Donlan, "Babies' Cottage"

Babies' Cottage is a beautifully restored building two blocks from my home in the Hastings-Sunrise neighbourhood of East Vancouver. Our neighbourhood association raises funds for the hospice with the very popular annual Trinity Street Christmas light show and celebration. Derek Von Essen's beautiful photographs of the building can be seen in *A Verse Map of Vancouver*, an anthology edited by George McWhirter (Vancouver: Anvil Press, 2009).

Tyler Enfield, "Six Times"

The poem began as fiction; an imagined conflict between imagined people. As always it's the images that drove it, forcing themselves onto the page from God knows where until the thing is done and I'm left scratching my jaw, marvelling at the sly precision of their relevance.

Jesse Ferguson, "Little 'o' Ode"

In the postmodern moment, we've become skeptical about grand poetic gestures. It's become difficult to write or to appreciate new poems that address "the big themes" of death, love, or religion head-on. In my poem "Little 'o' Ode" I attempt to avoid summarizing Beethoven's genius in its entirety. This particularizing approach, in this case, leading me to panegyrize the stick the composer used to hear his piano as he grew deaf, allows me (I hope) to both avoid an overly grand gesture and to convey my sense of humility.

Connie Fife, "A New World Poem"

"A New World Poem" is an illustration of what the Canada Council for the Arts stated about Connie Fife: "she has consistently used the power of the word to break through the barriers of injustice and intolerance."

Adam Getty, "Pender Harbour"

In the summer of 2007 I travelled to British Columbia to live in Pender Harbour for three months while I finished my most recent book, *Repose*. I had never been in such a small place so long, and was also ill. For the first few weeks I was nervous about my surroundings until one night I had a dream in which an old woman gave birth every night to a child and then "unmade" it by peeling its skin off, forcing me to watch in shackles and leg irons. I felt the dream reflected what I'd been writing about: the fact that maybe the natural world wasn't as benign as the poetic tradition might have us believe, but only seemed that way as a result of acclimatization, or something like it. Underneath the calm surface might be a writhing mass of biological activity, a kind of violent consumption, which made the environment what it is. Part of the inspiration for this, I confess, comes from Slavoj Zizek's essay "David Lynch and the Feminine Depression." This doesn't say all or even any of what I meant . . .

Steven Heighton, "Home Movies, 8 mm"

I wrote this poem pretty much straight up, just describing what I saw and felt while watching the old 8 mm footage that my father dug out of the crawlspace soon after my mother died in 2001. Frankly, I find it hard to think about how much I've failed to notice in my life. In some ways it's easier to write about it—especially in the second person.

Michael Johnson, "The Church of Steel"

My dad owns a milling machine from a World War II battleship. Patented in 1908. I've waited years to tell that. To tell how the belt chugged along like it might never die. How the bits gnawed away whatever I wanted to cut—how metal was a language I'd been taught since my toddling. Dad used to let me hold things, sometimes even try the taste of it all. So many scars, so much time pounding the panels of cars, torquing bolts—it hit me one day: I'd long lived in the church of steel. I had been writing poems with "church" titles—"The Church of My Mother's Hands," "The Church of Rot," "The Church of Thorn and Thicket" . . . —so I started with a title that intrigued me and just the word "knurl."

Grit in the oyster of my mouth. I couldn't let it go. I asked my dad what that trick with the lathe was called, and the width of the cut, and what it was all made of. And much like the projects of my growing up, I honed and trimmed and polished what felt like praise.

Sonnet L'Abbé, "Love Amid the Angloculture"

I am not great at writing love poems. This poem was an attempt to get at why, and it succeeds in a way I didn't expect. It is a loose, ragged poem; not satisfyingly resolved into a calm space where love, or these thoughts about it, live peacefully. I let the poem be as it is because it really does capture where my mind and gut feelings go when I start thinking about letting someone "in." This poem fights off the prospect of love in a move that seems as much about protecting the other as the self, and speaks the kind of love one is capable of when one still feels a toxicity inside. I look back on this poem and am happy to feel I wouldn't write it today. People can learn to filter their own waters.

Anita Lahey, "Man Tearing Down a Chimney"

The summer the chimney was rotting on the house on Cape Breton Island that I share with my parents, my cousin Shawn drove over one day in a pick-up truck packed with tools and equipment. Over a few hours, with a relentless focus and elegance that one might not expect to associate with destruction, he methodically and impressively knocked the thing down. I once wrote a magazine article about the destruction of an old Salvation Army hospital in Ottawa. This was like the small-scale, one-man version of that mammoth operation, and it felt important, as though the very act of making this part of the house disappear was a creation in itself, the next bit of plot in the ongoing history of our family, but without the ambiguity or emotional residue of human affairs, just something practical—noisy and messy and real, and happening right before my eyes.

M. Travis Lane, "The Confluence"

"The Confluence" reflects the experience of a morning walk I took while attending The Thin Air Literary Festival in Winnipeg. The unsettled history: Aboriginal, Métis, and European, and the new church built within the ruins of the old, are literally there. So, too, was the beggar.

Evelyn Lau, "The Night Market"

"The Night Market" came out of my failure to act with grace; instead, as usual, I assuaged my guilt by writing about the experience. The image of the impoverished old woman staring hungrily at the vats of food in the night market haunted me for months, as did my inability to help. I consoled myself with the fantasy that someone else, reading the poem, would remember it and, in the midst of plenitude, not let such an opportunity pass them by. The lines about the seagull came from what seemed a minor incident at the time; the wounded gull, its endurance of our hands on its body, reminded me of the experience of prostitution, which led to the deliberate line break in "I could buy her / a meal."

Richard Lemm, "Actaeon"

"Actaeon" had several textual promptings. First, two poems by an Australian friend, Fiona Papps: one a feminist re-telling of the Rapunzel tale, the other "Siren," a transgressive take on the mermaid who, in love with a man, wants to be human. As well, I'd devoured Atwood's *The Penelopiad* and Barry Unger's novel, *The Song of Kings*, which fleshes out the becalming of the Greek fleet en route to Troy and Agamemnon's odious sacrifice of Iphigenia to gain favourable winds. And I'd had my socks knocked off by Carol Ann Duffy's poems that draw on biblical and classical stories. Meanwhile, I'd been working (and still am) on a manuscript of love-and-sex poems, most of them emerging from varieties of erotic-romantic experience. "Actaeon" came from this confluence of more "personal" writing and texts that delved into and re-visioned old tales.

Dave Margoshes, "Becoming a Writer"

"Becoming a Writer" began with what I thought was a quote from Gabriel Garcia Marquez, something to the effect that "Everything I needed as a writer I had acquired by the time I was six." In fact, I used that quote, or what I thought may have only been a paraphrase, as an epigram to the poem, and it appeared that way in *Queen's Quarterly*. Later, as I was preparing for the publication of my new poetry collection, which includes that poem, I was unable to verify the quote—now I have no idea from whence it came— and dropped the epigram.

Don McKay, "Song for the Song of the Sandhill Crane"

Whether seen—flying or dancing—or heard, Sandhill Cranes speak directly to our earliest brains. In this they are like all cranes, as demonstrated vividly by Peter Matthiessen's

Birds of Heaven, and even more vividly by raw experience. The song originates in the Cretaceous and flows directly to us in the Anthropocene without deviating into either narrative or lyric.

Eric Miller, "Portrait of Hans Jaegger II (1943)"

Some of Edvard Munch's works appeal to me. I wanted to figure out why. Also, I have attempted to be a visual artist myself. The chance to mix an example of his lithography (or printing from stone) with a few of my phrases made me happy.

Shane Neilson, "Roadside Vegetable Stand, Outskirts of Kitchener"

This vegetable stand is just off Highway 7 on the road from Guelph to Kitchener. I used to work in Kitchener, and saw the stand in its many guises: lonely in winter, lonelier in summer. It is part of a larger farm, but the house is set far back from the road, too far to see. Cars rush past; it seems impossible that they once stopped on such a busy highway, looking for corn (I don't know why, but the expanse of fields, for some reason, has the ghosts of corn). I had the same feeling I imagined Philip Larkin did in "Church Going," and decided I'd steal one of his lines.

Peter Norman, "Super's Report"

I used to take my lunch break in the food court of an upscale Ottawa office block. I'd watch the building staff flit discreetly, murmuring into headsets, upholding an environment so varnished it was unsettling. One afternoon I returned to work with a pair of couplets scribbled on a serviette. The poem proceeded from there.

David O'Meara, "Café in Bodrum"

Bodrum was once the ancient city of Halicarnassus, ruled for a while by the Persian satrap Mausolus, whose tomb, the Mausoleum, was one of the Seven Wonders of the World. It's a seaside tourist town now. That atmosphere of history, and the present's rejection of it, haunted me.

P.K. Page, "Coal and Roses: A Triple Glosa"

I have for some years been in love with the glosa form. One day a friend sent me the Akhmatova three-stanza poem, "Everything is plundered . . ." And I wondered if I could write a triple glosa, moving from the worldly (grim) through nature to the sublime.

Elise Partridge, "Two Cowboys"

While walking in downtown Vancouver one day, I caught a glimpse of a man and child, looking like father and son, dressed identically and hurrying along, the father scowling and the boy struggling to keep up. I began this poem after the image kept returning to me over subsequent months.

Elizabeth Philips, "Before"

The line that serves as a kind of refrain here, "you can only get there by water," is the only line that remains from my original attempt to write about what must be a quintessential Canadian experience: sex outside. It took three years for me to attempt the poem again, and this time I decided to document, somewhat self-consciously, the line's journey through the poem. The poet Theodore Roethke has said that "Any fool can take a bad line out of a poem; it takes a real pro to throw out a good line." It is a great pleasure to resurrect one of those good lines, out of the many that remain as discards in all those pieces that never quite succeeded, those half-dreamed constructs, the writing of which helps the poet complete those few poems that *do* find their way at last into the reader's hands. In this way, the line is itself like memory, changing each time it appears in the poem, becoming enriched, and darkened, by its passage through time.

Meredith Quartermain, "Big News Café"

"Big News Cafe" is from Meredith Quartermain's most recent book, *Nightmarker* (NeWest), which explores the city as animal behaviour, museum and dream of modernity. In another recent book, entitled *Matter* (BookThug), she playfully riffs on Darwin's *Origin of Species* and *Roget's Thesaurus*. *Vancouver Walking* won the 2006 BC Book Award for Poetry. She is co-founder of Nomados Literary Publishers.

Matt Rader, "The Ocean Voyager"

"The Ocean Voyager" is a version of Arthur Rimbaud's "The Drunken Boat." It owes a debt to previous versions by Don McGrath and Steven Heighton. *The Ocean Voyager* was fished by John and Ralph Willson. It sank off the west coast of Vancouver Island in 1994. Not long after, John Willson passed. He was followed nine years later by his father, Ralph.

John Reibetanz, "To Darwin in Chile, 1835"

My wife and I love to read biographies aloud, and one of our most rewarding "finds" has been Janet Browne's splendid two-volume work on Charles Darwin. The poem grew out of our marvelling at he incongruity between Darwin's conservative social background and his ultimately revolutionary thinking. It focuses on one event that seemed, in retrospect, to pivot him from the one realm to the other, his experience of a massive earthquake in Chile while a young naturalist, long before his ideas on evolution developed. His experience of the earthquake embodies a recognition that our instabilities, not our permanencies, are what put us in harmony with the nature of the physical universe.

Robyn Sarah, "Echoes in November"

"Echoes in November" is about the mystery of resemblances—the fact that the world is full of things that remind us of other things. This subtle, lovely, sometimes spooky phenomenon is the root of metaphor, which is the stuff of poems and also of scientific theories. But often enough, our perception of these resemblances is fleeting, almost subliminal. They're like whispers. How many times must I have noticed that faint, tperfumy aftertaste at the top of a raw carrot, before I ever thought to put words to it?

Peter Dale Scott, "Breathing Exercise: A How-To Poem"

My Buddhist teacher Gil Fronsdal, trained in the traditions of both Zen and Vipassana, once taught me in retreat the technique of guiding my out-breath up the outside of my spine. I then spent half of three years in Thailand, where I developed this practice as a preliminary to my *metta* meditation. Frequently in this practice I am reminded of my remarkable poetry student Mark O'Brien (the subject of the Academy Award-winning short documentary *Breathing Lessons*). Mark was the quadriplegic survivor as a child of a crippling polio attack that left him struggling with every breath for the rest of his life. See his books *Breathing* and *The Man in the Iron Lung*.

Cora Siré, "Before Leaving Hué"

I wrote this as a ballad for Hué, a city that was a battleground during the war in Vietnam. I saw the scars of that war when I was there, a year after the US invasion of Iraq, and could not help but draw parallels. I also experienced the beauty of an old imperial city known for honouring its poets. When I met Thúy, a woman who weaves poetry into conical hats, I knew I would have to write about her. She embodies a Buddhist resilience, courage, and reverence for the healing powers of poetry that are the essence of Hué.

Karen Solie, "Tractor"

A few years ago, my parents bought a new tractor. It is so big they had to construct a new building to put it in. My relationship to it is complicated. The tractor is loud, it burns a lot of fuel, it's expensive to maintain. Machines like it are also necessary to making a living in prairie dryland farming. The poem's second stanza refers to a process by which American-owned (in this case) oil and gas companies drill for gas, a process fraught with hazards and awful byproducts, and one that fuels the tractor. Companies compensate farmers by way of small surface lease payments for the land disturbed by the drilling and truck traffic, a bit of money that helps some farmers continue to make a go of it. (And, since farmers have no mineral rights, if they were to say no to the companies, the companies would simply drill anyway and not pay them.) The tractor is implicated in all of this. It is also an astounding piece of machinery, a marvel of human ingenuity, and really fun to drive.

Carmine Starnino, "Pugnax Gives Notice"

Ten facts I couldn't fit into the poem. The "thumbs down" response—the audience's declaration of the death for a wounded fighter—is a myth (decision was left to a single judge). Most gladiators who died were between eighteen and twenty-five. Not all gladiators were bumped off; only criminals, the superstars were too profitable to die. Out-of-work Romans signed up to gladiator schools for the free food, clean lodgings, and medical care; in exchange, they agreed "to endure branding, chains, flogging or death by the sword." The Colosseum floor was sometimes flooded to create conditions for a sea-fight with gladiators fighting on the deck of ships. According to one story, twenty depressed gladiators committed group suicide rather than enter the arena. Emperor Trajan is responsible for the Colosseum's largest imperial show, which spanned 123 days and included 5,000 pairs of fighters. The gladiatorial games got their start as funeral rituals: combats were staged in honor of the deceased. Action figures of popular fighters could be purchased outside the arena. Some Romans believed gladiator blood cured epilepsy.

John Steffler, "Beating the Bounds"

I read somewhere about an ancient ritual in which once a year the elders of a community would take the young boys around to the points marking the boundaries of their parish or tribal territory and beat the boys at each of the boundary markers to make them remember their location. It seems to me that versions of this custom are still practised in the way societies indoctrinate their members with a sense of a home landscape and a home culture. I was thinking of Newfoundland and the way the markers that define its physical environment also define many aspects of its culture.

Ricardo Sternberg, "New Canaan"

These four poems are part of a sequence with, at present, no fixed name though with a working title of *The Monterey Songbook*. The poems are strung around a very general idea: that of a man, sitting on a bench facing the ocean and scrambling in his mind, memories of his life, of literature, and of Mexican TV dramas. Each poem in the sequence is made up of one long, meandering sentence. I am striving for a more colloquial style while keeping the language lively and taut.

John Terpstra, "The Highway That Became a Footpath"

The immediacy of the highway-building situation and the passion that the ones who climbed into trees showed for what seemed a hopeless cause, set against the long-range, nature/urban vision from the Book of Revelation, inspired me.

Sharon Thesen, "The Celebration"

The poem is a rant about being enjoined constantly to "celebrate" things that may be worthy, but not necessarily, of celebration. I got into a rhythm that invoked Ginsberg's "Howl," and I used a couple of lines I remembered (correctly, I hope) from Part II of his poem.

Matthew Tierney, "Nightingale"

Max is sensitive, supercilious, and pitiable; indulges egomaniacal Armageddon scenarios that decimate paralegals (among others, presumably) and make him the unlikeliest of action heroes; meanwhile works retail, the ghoulish p.m to a.m. shift, and spins off his hurt onto loved ones . . . sound like anybody you know? Call it a portrait of the artist. Tender is the night.

Patrick Warner, "O Brother"

This piece made an uneasy fit with the poems in my recently released book *Mole* and ended up on the print-shop floor. So I'm very happy that Al Moritz decided to pick it up, dust it off, and give it a new home.

Tom Wayman, "Teaching English"

Like many a contemporary writer, I have made a living much of my life teaching English at colleges and universities. I was reading the bio in somebody's book, which said they did the same work, and I began to muse about the phrase: "teaching English." The poem magically appeared. Not content with that, I've also written one called "Writing Poetry"—considering what I might communicate if I could actually write *to* the art form (published by the *The Literary Review of Canada*). Please stop me before I pun again.

Patricia Young, "July Baby"

Sex between humans is infinitely complex. "July Baby" is, I suppose, an attempt to look at this complexity in a less than serious manner. Writing it, I was reminded yet again that poetry can be play.

Changming Yuan, "Chinese Chimes: Nine Detours of the Yellow River"

Unlike most other authors of Asian origin, either born or raised in an English-speaking country, I did not begin to learn the alphabet in Shanghai until I was almost twenty. As essentially a Chinese cultural personality, I have thus always wanted to give English expression to something beyond Chinatown experiences or anti-communist sentimentalities. Inspired by a Chinese translation of *The God of Small Things*, which I happened to see on a student's bookshelf while tutoring him on the morning of February 4, 2006, "Nine Detours of the Yellow River" is one of the many China-related serial poems I have written. In this poem, I tried to portray the river as the mother river of the Chinese civilization: coincidently, the river has nine major detours, corresponding to the nine major dynasties in Chinese history since the Qin.

Jan Zwicky, "Practising Bach"

This poem was commissioned by Tafelmusik Baroque Orchestra and received its first performance in Toronto in January 2007, with Aisslinn Nosky on violin. For each movement, I read the relevant section of the poem, then Aisslinn played. It was a great gift to sense the synergy between the words, Bach's extraordinary music, and Aisslinn's own conception of the piece.

POET BIOGRAPHIES

MARGARET ATWOOD is the author of more than forty books—fiction, poetry, literary criticism, social history, and books for children. Her poetry collection, *The Circle Game*, won the Governor General's Award in 1966. Her novels include *The Handmaid's Tale*— winner of the Governor General's Award; *Alias Grace*—winner of the Giller Prize and the Premio Mondello in Italy; and *The Blind Assassin*—winner of the Man Booker Prize. Her most recent poetry collection, *The Door*, was published in 2007. *The Year of the Flood* (McClelland & Stewart, September 2009) is her latest novel. Margaret Atwood lives in Toronto with the writer Graeme Gibson.

MARGARET AVISON's work has, over the course of a career spanning four decades, won numerous awards, including two Governor General's Award and, for *Concrete and Wild Carrot*, the Griffin Poetry Prize. Her books of poetry include *Always Now: The Collected Poems* and *Momentary Dark*. Margaret Avison died in July 2007 in Toronto. Her final collection, *Listening: The Last Poems of Margaret Avison*, was published posthumously by McClelland & Stewart in spring, 2009.

KEN BABSTOCK is the author of *Mean* (1999), winner of the Atlantic Poetry Prize and Milton Acorn Award; *Days into Flatspin* (2001), winner of a K.M. Hunter Award and shortlisted for the Winterset Prize; and, most recently *Airstream Land Yacht* (2006), which was a finalist for the Governor General's Award, the Winterset Prize, the Griffin Prize, and won the Trillium Award for Poetry. All three of his collections were *Globe and Mail* Books of The Year. Babstock's poems have been translated into Dutch, German, French, and Serbo-Croatian. He lives in Toronto where he works as a writer, editor, and teacher.

SHIRLEY BEAR is a multimedia artist, writer, and traditional First Nation herbalist and Elder. Born on the Tobique First Nation, she is an original member of the Wabnaki language group of New Brunswick. She was the 2002 recipient of the New Brunswick Arts Board's Excellence in the Arts Award, and her writing has been included in several anthologies—including *The Colour of Resistance: A Contemporary Collection of Writing by Aboriginal Women* (Sister Vision, 1998). In 2006, McGilligan Books published her collection of art, poetry, and political writing, *Virgin Bones/Belayak Kcikug'nas'ikn'ug*.

TIM BOWLING has published several poetry collections, including *The Book Collector*; *Low Water Slack*; *Dying Scarlet* (winner of the 1998 Stephan G. Stephansson Award for poetry); *Darkness and Silence* (winner of the Canadian Authors Association Award for Poetry); *The*

Witness Ghost; and *The Memory Orchard* (both nominated for the Governor General's award). He is also the author of the novels, *Downriver Drift* (Harbour Publishing), *The Paperboy's Winter* (Penguin), and *The Bone Sharps* (Gaspereau Press). His nonfiction book, *The Lost Coast: Salmon, Memory and the Death of Wild Culture* (Nightwood Editions), was shortlisted for three literary awards and was chosen as a 2008 Kiriyama Prize "Notable Book." Bowling was awarded a Guggenheim Fellowship in 2008 and is the recipient of the Petra Kenney International Poetry Prize, the National Poetry Award, and the Orillia International Poetry Prize. A West Coast native, he now lives in Edmonton, Alberta.

ASA BOXER is a poet, literary critic, and teacher. His work won first prize in the 2004 CBC / *enRoute* poetry competition. And his debut book, *The Mechanical Bird*, won the Canadian Authors Association Poetry Prize. Boxer's work has been anthologized in several publications, including *The New Canon: An Anthology of Canadian Poetry* and the Oxford-Poetry Broadside Series. His poems, articles, and reviews have appeared in *Poetry London*, *Arc*, *Books in Canada*, *Maisonneuve*, and *Canadian Notes & Queries*.

ANNE COMPTON's most recent book is *asking questions indoors and out* (Fitzhenry & Whiteside, 2009). *Processional* (2005) won the Governor General's Award and the Atlantic Poetry Prize. *Opening the Island* (2002) also won the Atlantic Poetry Prize. Her critical works include *Meetings with Maritime Poets: Interviews* (2006). In 2008, Compton received the Alden Nowlan Award for Excellence in the Literary Arts.

JAN CONN's most recent volume of poetry is *Botero's Beautiful Horses* (Brick Books, 2009). Her other books include *Jaguar Rain* (Brick Books, 2006) and *Beauties on Mad River: Selected and New Poems* (Véhicule Press, 2000). Her work is included in *How the Light Gets In: An Anthology of Contemporary Poetry from Canada*, and has appeared in *Barrow Street*, *CV2*, *Dream Catcher*, *Poetry Ireland*, *The Malahat Review*, *The Massachusetts Review*, and *The Antigonish Review*. She won the inaugural (2006) *Malahat Review* P.K. Page Founders' Award Poetry Prize and a CBC Literary Award for poetry (2003). She lives in Great Barrington, MA, and studies the ecology and evolution of mosquitoes that transmit human pathogens at the Wadsworth Center, New York State Department of Health in Albany, NY. She travels frequently to Latin America. www.janconn.com

KEVIN CONNOLLY is a Toronto poet, editor and arts journalist. He has published four full-length collections, including *drift* (Anansi), which won the 2005 Trillium Poetry Award, and most recently, *Revolver* (Anansi, 2008). He is the poetry editor for Coach House books.

LORNA CROZIER's books have won the Governal General's, the Canadian Authors' Association, and two Pat Lowther Awards. A Distinguished Professor at the University of Victoria, she has published fourteen poetry collections, the most recent being *The Blue Hour of the Day*. She has received two honourary doctorates for her contribution to Canadian literature, her poems have been translated into several languages, and she has read her work around the world. A memoir, *Small Beneath the Sky*, was published by Greystone Books in 2009. Concurrently, a Spanish translation of her poems, *La Perspectiva del Gato* was published by Trilce Ediciones in Mexico City.

BARRY DEMPSTER is the author of fourteen books, including a novel, a children's book, two volumes of short stories, and ten collections of poetry. He has been nominated for the Governor General's Award twice and has won a Petra Kenney Award, a Confederation Poets' Prize, a *Prairie Fire* Poetry Contest, and the Canadian Authors' Association Chalmers Award for Poetry for his 2005 collection, *The Burning Alphabet*. In 2009, he published two new books of poetry: *Love Outlandish*, published by Brick Books, and *Ivan's Birches*, with Pedlar Press. Barry is senior editor at Brick Books. Over this past year, he was a Wired Writing mentor at the Banff Centre as well as facilitator of a two-week poetry workshop in Santiago, Chile.

DON DOMANSKI was born and raised on Cape Breton Island and now lives in Halifax, Nova Scotia. He has published eight books of poetry. In 2007 his book *All Our Wonder Unavenged* won the Governor General's Award and the Atlantic Poetry Prize, and in 2008 it also won the Lieutenant Governor of Nova Scotia Masterworks Arts Award. Published and reviewed internationally, his work has been translated into Czech, French, Portuguese, Arabic, and Spanish.

JOHN DONLAN is a native of Baysville, in Ontario's Muskoka region. He is a poetry editor at Brick Books. He spends half the year as a reference librarian at the Vancouver Public Library, and the other half writing poetry near Godfrey, Ontario. His collections of poetry are *Domestic Economy* (Brick Books, 1990, reprinted 1997), *Baysville* (House of Anansi Press, 1993), *Green Man* (Ronsdale Press, 1999), and *Spirit Engine* (Brick Books, 2008). He is also the author of *A Guide to Research @ Your Library* (Ontario Library Association/Vancouver Public Library, 2002).

TYLER ENFIELD was awarded the Writers' Federation Of New Brunswick Literary Prize for his upcoming book, *Wrush* (Greenleaf Book Group, 2010). He lives in Edmonton where he is the founding instructor of The Tinderbox, a writing workshop that encourages exploration into the origins of creativity. Visit at www.thetinderbox.ca

JESSE PATRICK FERGUSON was born in Cornwall, Ontario, and he is the author of five poetry chapbooks. He has contributed to publications such as: *Grain, Prairie Fire, The New Quarterly, Poetry Ireland Review, Harper's*, and *Poetry Magazine*. He is a poetry editor for *The Fiddlehead*, and he's a Celtic ballad collector, playing several musical instruments. His first full-length book of poems, *Harmonics*, was published in fall 2009 by Freehand Books.

CONNIE FIFE is Cree/Métis. Her poetry and critical writings have appeared in numerous anthologies and periodicals. She is the author of *Beneath the Naked Sun* (Sister Vision, 1992), *Speaking Through Jagged Rock* (Broken Jaw Press, 1999), and *Poems for a New World* (Ronsdale Press, 2001) She was also the editor of *The Colour of Resistance: A Contemporary Collection of Writing by Aboriginal Women* (Sister Vision, 1998), *Gatherings 2* (Theytus, 1991), and *Fireweed: Native Women's Issue* (1986). In 1999, she was one of four writers to receive the one-time Prince and Princess Edward Prize for Aboriginal Literature. Other awards include the University of British Columbia's Simon Lucas Award (1991) and the Pat Lackie Award (2002). Originally from Saskatchewan, she lives in Victoria, BC.

ADAM GETTY is the author of two books of poetry. His first book, *Reconciliation*, won the Gerald Lampert Memorial Award and the Hamilton Literary Award for Poetry, and was nominated for the Trillium Poetry Award. His second book, *Repose*, was published in 2008. He was recently nominated for the Premier's Award for Excellence in the Arts for an Emerging Artist. Adam attended the University of Toronto, where he studied anthropology, but left without taking a degree. He currently lives in Hamilton.

STEVEN HEIGHTON is the author of several poetry collections, including *The Ecstasy of Skeptics* and *The Address Book*, and the novels *The Shadow Boxer* and *Afterlands*, which has appeared in six countries, was a *New York Times Book Review* editors' choice, and was recently optioned for film. His poems and stories have appeared in *The London Review of Books*, *Poetry*, *Tin House*, *The Walrus*, *Europe*, *Agni*, *Poetry London*, *Brick*, and *Best English Stories*. Heighton has won several awards and has been nominated for the Governor General's Award, the Trillium Award, a Pushcart Prize, and Britain's W.H. Smith Award. A new novel, *Every Lost Country*, will appear in spring 2010, along with a poetry collection called *Patient Frame*.

MICHAEL JOHNSON was born in Bella Coola, British Columbia, and lives in Vancouver. His work has appeared in *The Fiddlehead*, *Prairie Fire*, *The Malahat Review*, *The Mid-American Review*, *Weber Studies*, and *The Southern Review*, among others, and was selected for *The Best American Poetry 2009*. He's been a Pushcart nominee and a finalist for the Ruth Lilly Fellowship and the Bronwen Wallace Award for Emerging Writers. He holds a BA in creative writing from Lewis-Clark State College, and is currently at work on a novel and a poetry manuscript.

SONNET L'ABBÉ is the author of two collections of poetry, *A Strange Relief* and, most recently, *Killarnoe*, both published by McClelland and Stewart. In 2000, she won the Bronwen Wallace Memorial Award for most promising writer under thirty-five, and in 1999 won The Malahat Review Long Poem Prize. L'Abbé has taught writing at the University of Toronto's School of Continuing Studies. She reviews poetry for the *Globe and Mail*, and is currently doing doctoral work in ecocritism and Romantic poetry at the University of British Columbia.

ANITA LAHEY is the author of the poetry collection *Out to Dry in Cape Breton* (Véhicule Press, 2006), which was nominated for the Trillium Book Award for Poetry and the Ottawa Book Award. The editor of *Arc Poetry Magazine*, she is also a journalist who has written on a wide range of topics for publications such as *The Walrus*, *Cottage Life*, *Maisonneuve*, *Canadian Geographic*, *Chatelaine*, the *Ottawa Citizen*, *Quill & Quire*, and several others. She lives in Montreal.

M. TRAVIS LANE, honorary research associate with the English department at the University of New Brunswick, honorary president of the Writers' Federation of New Brunswick, and life member of the League of Canadian Poets, has won numerous prizes, among them the Pat Lowther, the Atlantic Book Award, the Alden Nowlan Award for literary excellence, and the Bliss Carman. She has published ten books; her selected poems, *The Crisp Day Closing on my Hand*, came out in 2007; and Guernica Press plans to bring out this fall her eleventh collection, *The All-Nighter's Radio*.

EVELYN LAU was born in Vancouver in 1971. She is the author of nine books, including the bestselling *Runaway: Diary of a Street Kid*, published when she was eighteen, which was made into a CBC-TV movie. Her collections of poetry have been nominated for a Governor General's Award and won a Milton Acorn Award; her poems in literary magazines have been included in *The Best American Poetry* and won a National Magazine Award. Her most recent volume of poetry is *Treble* (Raincoast, 2005).

RICHARD LEMM teaches creative writing and Canadian and postcolonial literature at the University of Prince Edward Island. His most recent book, *Shape of Things to Come*, is a collection of short stories. A new book of poetry, *Burning House*, will be published in spring 2010 by Wolsak and Wynn.

DAVE MARGOSHES is a writer living in Regina. His stories and poems have been widely published in literary magazines and anthologies. His latest book, *Bix's Trumpet and Other Stories*, was named Book of the Year at the 2007 Saskatchewan Book Awards. A new book of poetry, *The Horse Knows the Way*, will be out in late 2009.

DON MCKAY's most recent books are *Strike/Slip* (McClelland & Stewart) and *The Muskwa Assemblage* (Gaspereau Press).

ERIC MILLER's most recent book is *The Day in Moss* (Fitzhenry & Whiteside, 2008). Previous books have been shortlisted for the ReLit Award and the Hubert Evans Prize. He is working on the second in a series of novels set in eighteenth-century Canada.

SHANE NEILSON published *Alden Nowlan and Illness* (Frog Hollow) in 2005. He is the author of *Exterminate My Heart* (Frog Hollow, 2009) and the trade book *My Manic Statement* (Biblioasis, 2009). *Complete Physical* is forthcoming in 2010 from The Porcupine's Quill.

PETER NORMAN's poems have appeared in numerous periodicals, as well as the anthologies *Jailbreaks: 99 Canadian Sonnets* and last year's inaugural edition of *The Best Canadian Poetry in English*. His first novel, *Emberton*, is forthcoming from Douglas & McIntyre, and he is also at work on a book of sonnets. He lives in Halifax.

DAVID O'MEARA was born and raised in Pembroke, Ontario. He now lives in Ottawa and tends bar at the Manx Pub. *Storm still* (1999) was shortlisted for the Gerald Lampert Award. *The Vicinity* (2003) was shortlisted for the Trillium Book Award for Poetry. *Noble Gas, Penny Black* (Brick Books, 2008) is his third collection.

P. K. PAGE was born in England and brought up on the Canadian prairies. She lived out of the country for many years with her diplomat husband, Arthur Irwin, and now resides in Victoria, British Columbia. She is the author of more than a dozen books of poetry, fiction, and nonfiction. Among other honours, she won the Governor General's Award for poetry for *The Metal and the Flower* (1954) and was made a Companion of The Order of Canada in 1998. She is also known as a visual artist, having exhibited her work at a number of venues in Canada and abroad. Her works are in permanent collections of the National Gallery of Canada and Art Gallery of Ontario. The Porcupine's Quill published her most recent poetry collection, *Coal and Roses*, in spring 2009.

ELISE PARTRIDGE's poems have appeared in Canadian, American, British, and Irish journals, including *The Fiddlehead, Riddle Fence, The New Yorker, Poetry, PN Review,* and *Poetry Ireland Review*. Her first book, *Fielder's Choice*, was shortlisted for the Gerald Lampert Award; her second, *Chameleon Hours*, was nominated for the Dorothy Livesay Poetry Prize and won the Canadian Authors Association Poetry Award. She has taught literature and writing and also works as an editor.

ELIZABETH PHILIPS is the author of four collections of poetry. Her most recent collection, *Torch River*, was released by Brick Books in spring 2007. She has taught creative writing in various programs across Canada, including all three of Banff's creative writing programs. She edits poetry and fiction for various publishers and is a former editor of the literary magazine *Grain*. She was recently appointed director of the Banff Centre's Writing with Style program for 2010. She lives in Saskatoon.

MEREDITH QUARTERMAIN developed a strong sense of place as a child that influenced her writing and remained with her during her studies at the University of British Columbia. She is the author of several poetry collections, including *Vancouver Walking*, which won the 2006 BC Book Prize for Poetry. She is also the co-founder of Nomados, a small literary press in Vancouver. Her latest collection, *Nightmarker*, was published by NeWest Press in September 2008.

MATT RADER, MFA (Oregon), is the author of two highly acclaimed books of poetry, *Miraculous Hours* (Nightwood, 2005) and *Living Things* (Nightwood, 2008), as well as the award-winning fine press chapbook, *The Land Beyond* (greenboathouse books, 2003). His poems and stories have appeared in journals across North America, Australia, and Europe and in anthologies such as *Breathing Fire 2: Canada's New Poets*, *The Journey Prize Anthology*, *The Echoing Years: Poetry from Canada and Ireland*, *Jailbreaks: 99 Canadian Sonnets*, and, most recently, *The Best Canadian Poetry in English 2008*.

JOHN REIBETANZ was born in New York City and grew up in the eastern United States and Canada. He put himself through university by working at numerous unpoetic jobs, and may be the only member of the League of Canadian Poets to have also belonged to the Amalgamated Meatcutters Union. He lives in Toronto with his wife and near their three grown children, and he teaches at Victoria College. His most recent collections are *Near Relations* (McClelland & Stewart, 2005) and *Transformations* (Goose Lane Editions, 2006).

ROBYN SARAH is the author of eight poetry collections, most recently *Pause for Breath* (2009), as well as two collections of short stories and a book of essays on poetry. Her poems have been published widely, anthologized, and broadcast in Canada and the United States. She lives in Montreal.

PETER DALE SCOTT, a former Canadian diplomat and professor of English at the University of California, Berkeley, is a poet, writer, and researcher. He is the author of the poetic trilogy *Seculum* (*Coming to Jakarta*, *Listening to the Candle*, *Minding the Darkness*) and, more recently, *Mosaic Orpheus* (2009), which includes "Breathing Exercise." In 2002 he received the Lannan Poetry Award. The former US poet laureate Robert Haas has written, "*Coming to Jakarta* is the most important political poem to appear in the English language in a very long time." Scott's website is www.peterdalescott.net.

CORA SIRÉ lives in Montreal and writes mainly of elsewheres, real and imaginary, in her poetry, essays, and fiction. She has released a CD of her poetry, thirteen poems with music, and is currently at work on a novel set in South America about a poet returning from exile.

KAREN SOLIE was born in Moose Jaw, and grew up on the family farm in southwest Saskatchewan. Her first collection of poems, *Short Haul Engine* (Brick Books, 2001), won the BC Book Prize Dorothy Livesay Award and was shortlisted for the Gerald Lampert Award and the Griffin Poetry Prize. Her second collection, *Modern and Normal* (Brick Books, 2005), was shortlisted for the Trillium Poetry Prize and included on the *Globe and Mail*'s list of the best books of 2005. Her third, *Pigeon*, was published in April 2009 by House of Anansi Press. She lives in Toronto with poet David Seymour.

CARMINE STARNINO is the author of four poetry collections, the latest of which is *This Way Out* (Gaspereau Press, 2009). He lives in Montreal, where he edits *Maisonneuve* magazine.

JOHN STEFFLER was Parliamentary Poet Laureate of Canada from 2006 to 2008. His books of poetry include *The Grey Islands*; *That Night We Were Ravenous*, winner of the Atlantic Poetry Prize; and *Helix: New and Selected Poems*, winner of the Newfoundland and Labrador Poetry Prize. Steffler is also the author of an award-winning novel, *The Afterlife of George Cartwright*. His newest collection of poems, *Lookout*, will be published by McClelland & Stewart in 2010.

RICARDO STERNBERG has published three books of poetry, *The Invention of Honey* (1990; republished 1996, 2006) and *Map of Dreams* (1996) with Véhicule Press, and *Bamboo Church* (2003; republished 2006) with McGill-Queens University Press. In 1998 Cyclops Press released, *Blindsight*, a CD of his readings. *Oriole Weather*, a Lyricalmyrical chapbook, was published in 2004 with illustrations by Mara Sternberg. He lives in Toronto.

JOHN TERPSTRA is the author of several poetry collections, including *Disarmament* (2003), a Governor General's Award nominee, and the Bressani Award-winning *Forty Days & Forty Nights* (1987). He is also an acclaimed prose author—*Falling Into Place* (2002) is his creative investigation of the Iroquois Bar, the geological formation that supports one of

Canada's busiest transportation corridors. His book, *The Boys, Or, Waiting For the Electrician's Daughter* (2005) was shortlisted for the Charles Taylor Prize and the BC Award for Canadian Non-Fiction. John Terpstra lives in Hamilton, Ontario, where he works as a writer and cabinetmaker.

SHARON THESEN is a poet and editor teaching in the Department of Creative Studies at UBC Okanagan in Kelowna, BC. She is a former editor of *The Capilano Review*, and editor of *The New Long Poem Anthology*. At UBC Okanagan she co-edits *Lake: a journal of arts and environment*. Her most recent book of poems is *The Good Bacteria*.

MATTHEW TIERNEY's second book, *The Hayflick Limit*, came out with Coach House Books in spring 2009. He is a recipient of a K.M. Hunter Award for Literature, and won first and second place in *This Magazine's* 2005 Great Canadian Literary Hunt. He continues to publish poems in journals and magazines across Canada, whenever they'll let him. He lives in Toronto.

PATRICK WARNER is the author of three collections of poetry. His latest collection, *Mole*, was published by House of Anansi Press in 2009. Originally from Claremorris, Co. Mayo, Ireland, he now lives in St. John's, Newfoundland.

TOM WAYMAN's poems have been published in more than fifteen collections in Canada and the US since 1973. His 2002 title, *My Father's Cup*, was shortlisted for both the Governor General's Award and the BC Book Prize for poetry. His latest book of poems is *High Speed Through Shoaling Water* (2007). Poems of his appeared in three 2009 anthologies: Nancy Holmes' *Open Wide a Wilderness: Canadian Nature Poems* (Wilfrid Laurier UP), George McWhirter's *A Verse Map of Vancouver* (Anvil), and John Bradley's *Eating the Pure Light: Homage to Thomas McGrath* (Backwaters). Wayman has edited several anthologies of poems, most recently *The Dominion of Love: An Anthology of Canadian Love Poems* (2001). His latest critical book is *Songs Without Price: The Music of Poetry in a Discordant World* (2008), based on a lecture he gave as the 2007 Ralph Gustafson Poetry Chair at the University of Vancouver Island. Since 2002 Wayman has taught English and writing at the University of Calgary. When not away working, he lives in the Selkirk Mountains of southeastern BC.

PATRICIA YOUNG has published nine collections of poetry. In 2008 she won *Arc's* Poem of the Year Contest, *Grain's* Prose Poem Competition, and was shortlisted for the CBC Literary Competition and *The Malahat Review's* Long Poem Contest. Her most recent collection of poems is *Here Come the Moonbathers* (Biblioasis, 2008). A new collection is forthcoming with Sono Nis Press in the spring of 2010.

CHANGMING YUAN grew up in rural China, published two books and many journal articles before moving to Canada, received his PhD in English from the University of Saskatchewan, and currently teaches writing in Vancouver. Since 2005, Yuan has had poetry appearing or forthcoming in more than 150 literary publications worldwide, including *Barrow Street*, *Canadian Literature*, and *London Magazine*. Although no Canadian publishers are willing enough yet to accept his work in a book form, Yuan's debut collection *Chansons of a Chinaman* is due out in the US from Leaf Garden Press in September 2009.

JAN ZWICKY has published seven collections of poetry, including *Songs for Relinquishing the Earth*, *Robinson's Crossing*, and, most recently, *Thirty-Seven Small Songs and Thirteen Silences*. Her books of philosophy include *Wisdom & Metaphor* and *Lyric Philosophy*, which will be reissued by Gaspereau Press in 2010. A native of Alberta, she now lives on the West Coast.

LONGLIST OF 50 POEMS

(in alphabetical order)

1. Abley, Mark. "Poppy Men." *The New Quarterly*. 106. 116.

2. Banks, Chris. "Darkening." *Arc*. 61. Winter 2009. 15.

3. Barton, John. "Study for a David and Goliath." *The Fiddlehead*. Summer 236. 110.

4. Besner, Linda. "Mort Besner." *Maisonneuve*. 29. Fall 2008. 33.

5. Borson, Roo. "Blowing Clouds." *The Malahat Review*. 165. Winter 2008. 62.

6. Boyle, Frances. "Momentum." *Arc*. 61. Winter 2009. 28.

7. Callanan, Mark. "Snowman." *Canadian Notes & Queries*. 75. 57.

8. Cayley, Kate. "Photograph: painter in her studio, 1907." *The Antigonish Review*. 155. Fall 2008. 111.

9. Clarke, George Elliott. "Autostrade per Los Angeles." *Vallum*. 6:1. 8.

10. Cole, Stewart. "The Freshly Made Bed." *Prism International*. 46:2. 54.

11. Cone, Tom and Jocelyn Morlock. "My Orange Thong." *The Capilano Review*. 3:4. 53.

12. Dalton, Mary. "Waste Ground." *The Fiddlehead*. Summer 236. 95.

13. Dodds, Jeramy. "Hoist Point." *The Fiddlehead*. Summer 236. 153.

14. Donaldson, Jeffery. "Enter, PUCK." *The New Quarterly*. 105. 18.

15. Donnelly, Richard. "Café," *PRECIPICe*. 16.1. 15.

16. Dumont, Marilyn. "Not Just a Platform for My Dance." *West Coast LINE*. 58. 39.

17. Enns, Karen. "Entering." *The Antigonish Review*. 153. 105.

18. Glenn, Lori Neilsen. "St. Boniface." *Contemporary Verse 2*. 31:2. 37.

19. Grubisic, Katia. "Prelude to Jumping in the River." *The Fiddlehead*. Spring 235. 50.

20. Guriel, Jason. "Shopping Cart, Abandoned on Front Lawn." *Canadian Notes & Queries*. 75. 55.

21. Harper, Jennica. "Liner Notes." *Prism International*. 47:1. 40.

22. Hunter, Aislinn. "And Then We Let Ourselves In." *Room*. 3:2. 79.

23. Hunter, Rose. "Jesse." *Contemporary Verse 2*. 30:4. 40.

24. Jerome, Gillian. "Unknown Girl from Bountiful." *Grain*. 35:3. 20.

25. Johnstone, Jim: "Field Note—Cliff Diving." *The Malahat Review*. 163. Summer 2008. 52.

26. Jollimore, Troy. "Regret." *The Walrus*. December 2008. 63.

27. Lambert, Sandra. "Fleshy Mystery." *Contemporary Verse 2*. 30:3. 95.

28. Leedahl, Shelley A. "Trivialities (Designing a Future)." *Grain*. 35:4. 39.

29. Lista, Michael. "Fidelity." *The Malahat Review*. 163. Summer 2008. 75.

30. Mac, Kathy. "Isabella, Double-You Be." *Event*. 37:1. 37.

31. Martin, Mathew. "Aesthetic Distance." *Contemporary Verse 2*. 30:3. 72.

32. McCaffery, Steve. "Still Life with radishes and counter intelligence." *PRECIPICe*. 16:1. 20.

33. McCartney, Sharon. "Against Scaffolding." *Queen's Quarterly*. 115:1. 153.

34. McElrea, Karen. "The Long Way Home." *Freefall*. XVIII:2. 24.

35. Munro, Jane. "Child with Two Adults." *The Antigonish Review*. 155. Fall 2008. 85.

36. Musgrave, Susan. "La Oscura." *The Literary Review of Canada*. 16:7. 19.

37. Nason, Jim. "Narcissus Unfolding." *Contemporary Verse 2*. 30:3. 22.

38. Newman, Daniel. "The Hawk." *The Antigonish Review*. 154. 120.

39. Pacey, Mike. "Snack Foods: a Semiotics." *Prairie Fire*. 29:1. 66.

40. Queyras, Sina. "The Endless Path of the New." *The Capilano Review*. 3:6. 66.

41. Richardson, Peter. "At Carruthers Point." *The Malahat Review*. 164. Fall 2008. 48.

42. Safarik, Allan. "Foreclosure." *Freefall*. XVIII:2. 46.

43. Slegtenhorst, Hendrik. "Touring With Charles." *Contemporary Verse 2*. 31:1. 40.

44. Solway, David. "Envoi." *The New Quarterly*. 106. 117.

45. Struthers, Betsy. "Harvest Moon: September." *Descant*. 141. Summer 2008. 165.

46. Swift, Todd. "The Afternoon Drinkers." *Event*. 36:3. 69.

47. Taylor, Regan. "Parc des Hommes-Forts." *The New Quarterly*. 106. 100.

48. Thran, Nick. "Aria with a Mirror and No Earplugs." *Event*. 37:3. 65.

49. Wynand, Derk. "Table Talk." *The Malahat Review*. 163. Summer 2008. 79.

50. Zieroth, David. "Insurance." *Event*. 36:3. 44.

MAGAZINES CONSIDERED FOR THE 2009 EDITION

The Antigonish Review

PO Box 5000
Antigonish, NS B2G 2W5
Tel: (902) 867-3962
Fax: (902) 867-5563
Email: tar@stfx.ca
http://www.antigonishreview.com/

Arc: Canada's National Poetry Magazine

PO Box 81060
Ottawa, ON K1P 1B1
http://www.arcpoetry.ca/

Ascent Aspirations Magazine

http://www.ascentaspirations.ca

Brick: A Literary Journal

Box 609, Stn. P
Toronto, ON M5S 2Y4
http://www.brickmag.com/

Books in Canada
[Ceased publication]
http://www.booksincanada.com/

Canadian Literature

University of British Columbia
1866 Main Mall–E158
Vancouver, BC V6Y 1Z1
Tel: (604) 822-2780
Fax: (604) 822-5504
E-mail: can.lit@ubc.ca
http://www.canlit.ca/

Canadian Notes & Queries

PO Box 92
Emerville, ON N0R 1A0
Tel: (519) 968-2206
Fax: (519) 250-5713
Email: info@notesandqueries.ca
http://www.notesandqueries.ca/

Carousel

UC 274 University of Guelph
Guelph, ON N1G 2W1
Email: carouselbook@yahoo.ca
http://www.carouselmagazine.ca/

The Capilano Review

2055 Purcell Way
North Vancouver, BC V7J 3H5
Tel: (604) 984-1712
Email: contact@thecapilanoreview.ca
http://www.thecapilanoreview.ca/

Cerulean Rain

www.ceruleanrain.com

Contemporary Verse 2: The Canadian Journal of Poetry and Critical Writing

207–100 Arthur St.
Winnipeg, MB R3B 1H3
Tel: (204) 949-1365
Fax: (204) 942-5754
E-mail: cv2@mts.net
http://www.contemporaryverse2.ca/

Dalhousie Review

Dalhousie University
Halifax, NS B3H 4R2
Tel: (902) 494-2541
Fax: (902) 494-3561
Email: dalhousie.review@dal.ca
http://dalhousiereview.dal.ca/

Descant

PO Box 314, Stn. P
Toronto, ON M5S 2S8
Email: info@descant.ca
http://www.descant.ca/

Ditch

http://ditchpoetry.com

enRoute Magazine

Spafax Canada
4200 boul. St-Laurent, Ste. 707
Montreal, QC H2W 2R2
Tel: (514) 844-2001
Fax: (514) 844-6001
http://www.enroutemag.com/

Event

P.O. Box 2503
New Westminster, BC V3L 5B2
Tel: (604) 527-5293
Fax: (604) 527-5095
E-mail: event@douglas.bc.ca
http://event.douglas.bc.ca/

Exile Quarterly

Exile/Excelsior Publishing Inc.
134 Eastbourne Ave.
Toronto, ON M5P 2G6
http://www.exilequarterly.com/quarterly/

Existere: Journal of Arts and Literature

Vanier College 101E
York University
4700 Keele Street
Toronto, ON M3J 1P3
Email: existere.journal@gmail.com
http://www.yorku.ca/existere/

The Fiddlehead

Campus House, 11 Garland Court
University of New Brunswick
PO Box 4400
Fredericton, NB E3B 5A3
Tel: (506) 453-3501
Fax: (506) 453-5069
Email: fiddlehd@unb.ca
http://www.lib.unb.ca/Texts/Fiddlehead/

Filling Station

PO Box 22135, Bankers Hall
Calgary, AB T2P 4J5
http://www.fillingstation.ca/

FreeFall Magazine

922–9th Ave. SE
Calgary AB T2G 0S4
Email: freefallmagazine@yahoo.ca
http://www.freefallmagazine.ca/

Grain Magazine

PO Box 67
Saskatoon, SK s7k 3k1
Tel: (306) 244-2828
Fax: (306) 244-0255
Email: grainmag@sasktel.net
http://www.grainmagazine.ca/

Hammered Out
[Ceased publication]
http://hammeredoutlitzine.blogspot.com

The Leaf

The Brucedale Press
Box 2259
Port Elgin, ON, noh 2c0

Literary Review of Canada

PO Box 8, Stn. K
Toronto, ON m4p 2g1
Email: poetry@lrcreview.com
http://lrc.reviewcanada.ca/

Maisonneuve Magazine

4413 Harvard Ave.
Montreal, QC h4a 2w9
Tel: (514) 482-5089
http://www.maisonneuve.org/

The Malahat Review

University of Victoria
PO Box 1700, Station CSC
Victoria, BC v8w 2y2
Tel: (250) 721-8524
Fax: (250) 472-5051
Email: malahat@uvic.ca
http://malahatreview.ca

Maple Tree Literary Supplement

http://www.mtls.ca

Matrix Magazine

1400 de Maisonneuve W., Ste. LB-658
Montreal, QC h3g 1m8
Email: info@matrixmagazine.org
http://www.matrixmagazine.org/

Misunderstandings Magazine

178 Lawrence Ave. E.
Toronto, ON m4n 1t1
Email: misunderstandings.magazine@
    gmail.com
http://www.misunderstandingsmagazine.
    com/

The Nashwaak Review

St. Thomas University
Fredericton, NB E3B 5G3
Phone: (506) 452-0426
Fax: (506) 450-9615
Email: tnr@stu.ca
http://w3.stu.ca/stu/about/publications/
    nashwaak/nashwaak.aspx

The New Quarterly

St. Jerome's University
290 Westmount Rd. N.
Waterloo, ON N2L 3G3
http://www.tnq.ca/

Northern Poetry Review

http://www.northernpoetryreview.com/

Other Voices

Box 52010, 8210–109 St
Edmonton, AB T6G 2T5
http://www.othervoices.ca/

Ottawater

http://www.ottawater.com/

Peter F Yacht Club

858 Somerset Street West
Main floor
Ottawa, ON K1R 6R7
Email: rob_mclennan@hotmail.com
http://www.abovegroundpress.blogspot.
   com/

Poetry Studio

http://www.studiopoetry.ca/

Prairie Fire

Prairie Fire Press, Inc.
423–100 Arthur St.
Winnipeg, MB R3B 1H3
Tel: (204) 943-9066
Fax: (204) 942-1555
Email: prfire@mts.net
http://www.prairiefire.ca/about.html

PRECIPICe

Department of English Language and
   Literature
Brock University
500 Glenridge Ave.
St. Catharines, ON L2S 3A1
http://www.brocku.ca/precipice/

PRISM International

Creative Writing Program
University of British Columbia
Buch. E462–1866 Main Mall
Vancouver, BC V6T 1Z1
Tel: (604) 822-2514
Fax: (604) 822-3616
http://prism.arts.ubc.ca/

Queen's Quarterly

Queen's University
144 Barrie St.
Kingston, Ontario K7L 3N6
Tel: (613) 533-2667
Fax: (613) 533-6822
Email queens.quarterly@queensu.ca
http://www.queensu.ca/quarterly

QWERTY

c/o English Department
University of New Brunswick
PO Box 4400
Fredericton, NB E3B 5A3
Email: qwerty@unb.ca
http://www.lib.unb.ca/Texts/QWERTY/

Rampike

English Department
University of Windsor
401 Sunset Ave.
Windsor, ON N9B 3P4
http://web4.uwindsor.ca/rampike

Rhythm

http://rhythmpoetrymagazine.english.
    dal.ca/

Room

PO Box 46160, Stn. D
Vancouver, BC V6J 5G5
Email: contactus@roommagazine.com
http://www.roommagazine.com/

subTERRAIN

PO Box 3008, MPO
Vancouver, BC V6B 3X5
Tel: (604) 876-8710
Fax: (604) 879-2667
Email: subter@portal.ca
http://www.subterrain.ca/

Taddle Creek

PO Box 611, Stn. P
Toronto, ON M5S 2Y4
Email: editor@taddlecreekmag.com
http://www.taddlecreekmag.com/

THIS Magazine

401 Richmond St. W., #396
Toronto, ON M5V 3A8
Editorial Tel: (416) 979-8400
Business Tel: (416) 979-9429
Fax: (416) 979-1143
Email: info@thismagazine.ca
http://www.thismagazine.ca/

The Toronto Quarterly

http://thetorontoquarterly.blogspot.com/

Vallum

PO Box 326, Westmount Stn.
Montreal, QC H3Z 2T5
Tel/Fax: (514) 237-8946
http://www.vallummag.com/

The Walrus

19 Duncan St., Ste. 101
Toronto, ON M5H 3H1
Tel: (416) 971-5004
Fax: (416) 971-8768
Email: info@walrusmagazine.com
http://www.walrusmagazine.com/

West Coast LINE

2027 East Annex
8888 University Drive
Simon Fraser University
Burnaby, BC V5A 1S6
Tel: (604) 291-4287
Fax: (604) 291-4622
Email: wcl@sfu.ca
http://www.westcoastline.ca/

White Wall Review

Ryerson Literary Society
c/o Department of English
5th floor, Jorgenson Hall
350 Victoria St.
Toronto, ON M5B 2K3
http://www.ryerson.ca/wwr/

Windsor Review

Department of English
University of Windsor
401 Sunset
Windsor, ON N9B 3P4
Tel: (519) 253-3000, ext 2290
Fax: (519) 971-3676
Email: uwrevu@uwindsor.ca
http://windsorreview.wordpress.com/

PERMISSION ACKNOWLEDGEMENTS

Tightrope Books gratefully acknowledges the authors and publishers for permission to reprint the following copyrighted works:

"Ice Palace" from *The Door: Poems* by Margaret Atwood copyright © 2007 by O.W. Toad Ltd. Used with permission of the publishers. Published in Canada by McClelland & Stewart Ltd. Published internationally by Virago, an imprint of Little, Brown Book Group. Published in the USA by Houghton Mifflin. Reprinted by permission of Houghton Mifflin Harcourt Publishing Company. All rights reserved. "Ice Palace" appeared in *Descant* (142, p. 34).

"Two Whoms or I'm in Two Minds" from *Listening: The Last Poems of Margaret Avison* by Margaret Avison copyright © 2009. Published by McClelland & Stewart Ltd. "Two Whoms or I'm in Two Minds" originally appeared in *Brick* (81, p. 38). Used with permission of the publisher.

"Autumn News from The Donkey Sanctuary" originally appeared in *The Fiddlehead* (239, p. 152) copyright © 2008 by Ken Babstock. Used with permission of the author.

"Flight" appeared in *West Coast LINE* (58, p. 110) copyright © 2008 by Shirley Bear. An earlier version of "Flight" was published in Shirley Bear's *Virgin Bones* (McGilligan Books, 2006). Used with permission of the author.

"1972" from *The Book Collector* copyright © 2008 by Tim Bowling. Reproduced with permission from Nightwood Editions. www.nightwoodeditions.com. "1972" originally appeared in *The Fiddlehead* (236, p. 46).

"Dante's Ikea" originally appeared in *Arc* (60, p. 80) copyright © 2008 by Asa Boxer. Used with permission of the author.

"Even Now" from *Asking Questions Indoors and Out* copyright © 2008 by Anne Compton. Reproduced with permission from Fitzhenry & Whiteside. "Even Now" originally appeared in the *Literary Review of Canada* (16.8, p. 17).

"Space Is a Temporal Concept" originally appeared in the *Literary Review of Canada* (16.5, p. 15) copyright © 2008 by Jan Conn. Used with permission of the author.

"Last One on the Moon" from *Revolver* by Kevin Connolly copyright © 2008. Published by House of Anansi. Reprinted with permission of the publisher. "Last One on the Moon" originally appeared in *Maisonneuve* (25).

"Mercy" originally appeared in *Vallum* (6.1, p. 52) copyright © 2008 by Lorna Crozier. Used with permission of the author.

"Groin" originally appeared in *Canadian Literature* (195, p. 102) copyright © 2008 by Barry Dempster. Used with permission of the author.

"Bite Down Little Whisper" originally appeared in *Prairie Fire* (29.4, p. 19) copyright ©
2008 by Don Domanski. Used with permission of the author.

"Babies' Cottage" from *Spirit Engine* by John Donlan © copyright 2008. Published by Brick
Books. Used with permission of the publisher. "Babies' Cottage" originally appeared in
Event (36.3, p. 76).

"Six Times" originally appeared in *Grain* (36.1, p. 76) copyright © 2008 by Tyler Enfield.
Used by permission of the author.

"Little 'o' Ode" originally appeared in *The Dalhousie Review* (88.1, p. 147) copyright © 2008
by Jesse Ferguson. Used with permission of the author.

"A New World Poem" originally appeared in *West Coast LINE* (58, p. 130) copyright © 2008
by Connie Fife. Used with permission of the author.

"Pender Harbour" from *Repose* copyright © 2008 by Adam Getty. Reproduced with
permission from Nightwood Editions. www.nightwoodeditions.com. "Pender Harbour"
originally appeared in *Hammered Out* (13, p. 34).

"Home Movies, 8mm" from *Patient Frame* copyright © 2010 by Steven Heighton.
Reproduced with permission from House of Anansi Press, Toronto. "Home Movies,
8mm" originally appeared in *The New Quarterly* (105, p. 12).

"The Church of Steel" originally appeared in *Queen's Quarterly* (115.4, p. 634) copyright ©
2008 by Michael Johnson. Used with permission of the author.

"Love Amid the Angloculture" originally appeared in *West Coast LINE* (59, p. 130) copyright
© 2008 by Sonnet L'Abbé. Used with permission of the author.

"Man Tearing Down a Chimney" originally appeared in *The Antigonish Review* (155, p. 9)
copyright © 2008 by Anita Lahey. Used with permission of the author.

"The Confluence" originally appeared in *Prairie Fire* (29.3, p. 48) copyright © 2008 by
M. Travis Lane. Used with permission of the author.

"The Night Market" originally appeared in *subTerrain* (50, p. 48) copyright © 2008 by
Evelyn Lau. Used with permission of the author.

"Actaeon" originally appeared in *The Fiddlehead* (237, p. 36) copyright © 2008 by Richard
Lemm. Used with permission of the author. "Actaeon" will also be published in Richard
Lemm's forthcoming collection, *Burning House*, (Wolsak and Wynn 2010).

"Becoming a Writer" from *The Horse Knows the Way* by Dave Margoshes copyright © 2009.
Published by BuschekBooks 2009. "Becoming a Writer" originally appeared in *Queen's*

"Before Leaving Hué" originally appeared in *Descant* (141, p. 180) copyright © 2008 by Cora Siré. Used with permission of the author.

"Tractor" from *Pigeon* copyright © 2009 by Karen Solie. Reproduced with permission from House of Anansi Press, Toronto. "Tractor" originally appeared in *The Walrus* (March 2008, p. 67).

"Pugnax Gives Notice" originally appeared in *Arc* (60, p. 37) copyright © 2008 by Carmine Starnino. Used with permission of the author.

"Beating the Bounds" from *Lookout* by John Steffler copyright © 2010. Published by McClelland & Stewart Ltd. "Beating the Bounds" originally appeared in the *Literary Review of Canada* (16.8, p. 17). Used with permission of the publisher.

"New Canaan" originally appeared in the *Literary Review of Canada* (16.8, p. 17) copyright © 2008 by Ricardo Sternberg. Used with permission of the author.

"The Highway That Became a Footpath" originally appeared in *The Fiddlehead* (234, p. 81) copyright © 2008 by John Terpstra. Used with permission of the author.

"The Celebration" originally appeared in *The Capilano Review* (3.5, p. 25) copyright © 2008 by Sharon Thesen. Used with permission of the author.

"Nightingale" from *The Hayflick Limit* copyright © 2009 by Matthew Tierney. Reproduced with permission from Coach House Books. "Nightingale" originally appeared in *Prairie Fire* (29.2, p. 105).

"O Brother" originally appeared in *The Fiddlehead* (236, p. 78) copyright © 2008 by Patrick Warner. Used with permission of the author.

"Teaching English" by Tom Wayman, *High Speed Through Shoaling Water*, Harbour Publishing, 2007. Reproduced with permission from the publisher. "Teaching English" appeared in *Queen's Quarterly* (115.3, p. 473).

"July Baby" originally appeared in *Maisonneuve* (27, p. 41) copyright © 2008 by Patricia Young. Used with permission of the author.

"Chinese Chimes: Nine Detours of the Yellow River" originally appeared in *The Nashwaak Review* (20/21.1, p. 87) copyright © 2008 by Changming Yuan. Used with permission of the author.

"Practising Bach" originally appeared in *Vallum* (6.1, p. 20) copyright © 2008 by Jan Zwicky. Used with permission of the author.

ACKNOWLEDGEMENTS

Tightrope Books would like thank all the poets whose work appears here and on the longlist. A special thank you to all the literary journals and magazines that kindly gave us subscriptions for the guest editor to draw from for *The Best Canadian Poetry in English 2009*. Tightrope Books is particularly grateful to those journal editors who helped us locate poets and poems. Thank you to Shelley Adler for use of her art for the cover, and to publishers' rights and permissions departments for their generous assistance. Thanks to Joe Saturnino at Revival, Stephanie Bolster, David Lehman, and Marilyn Biederman. Finally, a big thank you to guest editor A.F. Moritz, series editor Molly Peacock, and managing editor Heather Wood.

A.F MORITZ has written more than ten books of poetry, has been a finalist for the Governor General's Award, and has won the Award in Literature of the American Academy of the Arts and a Guggenheim Fellowship. He recently won *Poetry* magazine's Bess Hokin Prize for his poem "The Sentinel." His latest book, *The Sentinel*, was shortlisted for the Governor General's Award and won the 2009 Griffin Poetry Prize. He lives in Toronto and teaches at Victoria University.

MOLLY PEACOCK is the author of six volumes of poetry, including *The Second Blush* (McClelland and Stewart) and *Cornucopia: New and Selected Poems* (W.W. Norton and Company/Penguin Canada). She is the poetry editor of the *Literary Review of Canada*. Before the emigrated to Canada in 1992, she was one of the creators of Poetry in Motion on the Buses and Subways in New York City, and she served as an early advisor to Poetry on the Way. She is also the author of a memoir *Paradise, Piece by Piece* and *How to Read a Poem and Start a Poetry Circle*. Anthologized in *The Best of the Best American Poetry* and the *Oxford Book of American Poetry*, her poems have appeared in *The Paris Review*, *The New Yorker*, the *TLS*, and other leading literary journals. Recently she toured with her one-woman show in poems, "The Shimmering Verge," produced by the London, Ontario-based company, Femme Fatale Productions. She lives in Toronto with her husband, Michael Groden, an English professor at the University of Western Ontario. Her website is www.mollypeacock.org.